UFO-UK Updated

By
Peter Paget

PETER PAGET

UFO UK Updated

© Peter Paget 2018
All Rights Reserved
peterpaget2012@yahoo.co.uk

ISBN-13: 978-1720467007
ISBN-10: 1720467005

All rights reserved. No part of this publication may be reproduced, distributed, or transmitted in any form or by any means, including photocopying, recording, or other electronic or mechanical methods, without the prior written permission of the publisher, except in the case of brief quotations embodied in critical reviews and certain other non-commercial uses permitted by copyright law.

Original version published by, 1980 New English Library Edition.

Rewritten and updated 2018

PETER PAGET

Also by Peter Paget:

The Welsh Triangle (Five Editions Granada, Panther, Grafton, 1979-1989)
UFO UK 1980 (New English Library Edition)
UFO UK Updated (2018 paperback and eBook editions)
Secret Life of a Spook (2016 Paperback & E-book editions)
The Welsh Triangle Revisited (Paperback & E-book editions 2018)

Contributed to:

The Ufonauts (1979 Panther),
The Uninvited (1979 Star)
Crop Circles Revealed (2001 USA Edition)

Coming soon:

The Dark Triangle (Expected 2019)

UFO UK - UPDATED

ACKNOWLEDGEMENTS

The collation of this book owes much to the kind cooperation of some 3,500 sincere and intelligent British citizens who have diligently told me their observations over the past years.

Special mention to Ed Harris, Maureen, Keith, Denise, Tony, Irene, Colin and Kevin for their research assistance at various times. Extracts from articles and letters referred to in the text appear by kind permission of the Fountain Journal and its contributors. It is regrettable that the Journal ceased publication in 1977 and is now no longer available to readers in print but is still available online.

I would particularly like to thank my friend and colleague (the late) Professor Hans Holzer, of New York, for his encouragement of our work over the decades.

Sincere gratitude also to Pauline Penn, Jean Matthews, Tania T, Paul Georgian, Lloyd Canning, Col. John Paul Forrestal (USAF Retired) and also to my former wife Jane for secretarial, editorial and research assistance. I would also like to deeply thank my friends, family and my wife (A) tolerating me taking time to assemble this complicated and time-consuming manuscript all over again.

Special mention too of the dedication and loyalty of all the past and present members of NAIG (North Atlantic Intelligence Group) for their devotion to 'The Truth, The Truth, and Nothing But The Truth.' They were 132, now just four good men. Blessings to those skyward bound who gave years of service to crown and country here and overseas. Special Mention goes to Major R, Sgt C & the late Col E.M.

The original book, as is this updated version, is dedicated to all those lonely witnesses of the incredible, in this most curious of mysterious worlds.

In memorandum to James Vincent Forrestal (1892–1949) the last Cabinet-level United States Secretary of the Navy and the first United States Secretary of Defence; who gave his life in the pursuit of transparency and honesty in government. R.I.P.

Contents

Acknowledgements 5
Contents 7
Prologue 2018 9
Chapter 1: From Capital to Coastline 13
Chapter 2: East Anglian Enigmas 34
Chapter 3: Middle England And The North Sky 52
Chapter 4: The Warminster 'Thing' 69
Chapter 5: Hampshire Happenings 99
Chapter 6: Behind The Welsh Triangle 117
Chapter 7: Mystery Of The Moors 137
Chapter 8: UFO Cults And Societies 148
Chapter 9: Why The 'Cover-Up'? 168
Chapter 10: Inner or outer space? 186
Chapter 11: Dead men talk 228
Postscript: UFO – original Update 1980 240
Epilogue 2018: 'Brave New World' 243
Where to find Peter online 246
Other books by Peter Paget 247

"I think me are property.
I say we belong to something.
That once upon a time this earth was a no-man's
land: That other worlds explored and colonised
here and fought among themselves for possession.
But now it is owned by something
and that something owns this earth
and all others have been warned off."

Charles Fort

(August 6, 1874 – May 3, 1932)

Prologue 2018

In updating this important survey of the UFO scene back in the 1970s to the 21st Century, I have not continued to diarise the endless stream of day-to-day reports of UFOs in our skies. For indeed, all the activity that was sampled in this detailed study of the late 70s has continued unabated. They have not gone away. Some years have seen more reports than others, but in the main, the profiles have remained the same.

In fact, there is a remarkable continuity in the style and nature of the operations reported, both by civilians and the military. I am deeply grateful to the members of NAIG, as referenced in the acknowledgments, for continuing to provide me with 'insider' data, not in the public domain. Where I can, I have married this with already exposed information and, on important points, merged both data streams together to give a comprehensive and understandable picture.

I have gone through the 1980 edition, adding to it and rewriting as I went along. Additionally, I have supplemented further items that would not have easily fitted into the earlier dialogue. The amazing thing upon this revision is how much we actually 'knew' back then, without being able to see it. Hidden in plain sight, as we say in intelligence.

I say 'we' because, as you will already know if you have read my 2016 autobiography, *Secret Life of a Spook*, now that I am 'retired' I can reveal the other reason for my interest in all matters extra-terrestrial. Namely, that I served for many years in the employ of Intelligence services, both British and Internationally. You will understand therefore, that as I was still on 'active duties' at the time of writing the original manuscript, I could not permit any hint of my former 'double-life' to be revealed. Therefore, some of the information I knew had to be kept out of the book at that time, but I can now reveal it in this updated edition.

Back when I was writing *The Welsh Triangle*, (now similarly updated in a new edition, *The Welsh Triangle Revisited*), I was rather 'starry-eyed' and taken up by all the atmosphere and the culture of the 1970s. I have always sought to find and bring out of the data the very best interpretation that was possible and advise people accordingly. I realise now that over the years, I too was 'compartmentalised' and that I can now give a more balanced and accurate analysis of what the real situation is and indeed has been for a very long time.

In short, there are two time-streams to this planet that have played out here and continue to do so—

both with their own, very different, agendas. In the overview of both recent and ancient history, at various times the Earth has been influenced by one or other of what you might call 'more positive' 'or more negative' exploitative groups. It's a bit like the changing of political parties in governments that oscillate between one view and another.

Ironically, you can trace this right back to the creators of the modern human race, Cro-Magnon man, who were the 'helpers' to the 'gods' in their gold mining operations in Africa. In those days, the dissident members of the workforce were cast out, exiled to meet their doom in the unfriendly wilds and jungles of a very green and fertile World. The two, related imperial leaders of the ruling elite disagreed on the fate of the 'rebels'. One king wanted to exterminate them to solve the problem, the other avowed that they should just be left alone to die out naturally. They did not. They survived, evolved and eventually became modern man as we know him today.

The dichotomy of these two attitudes is mirrored today in the two philosophical attitudes of the 'off-world' and 'within-world' groups. They continue to interact both with humankind and with our planet, as a sustainable resource to their own isolated and separate civilisations, sharing this binary Earth/Lunar system and the whole solar system within which Earth resides. For millennia, the secret of this co-existence has been keep from all but the initiates and the elites, no matter upon which side they fall, as the operations of these so-called 'ETs' are best served if you the general public think, or are encouraged to think, that they don't exist. 'They Live'; to refer to a popular cult film.

In reviewing the data in the original publication of UFO UK, the activities and modus operandi of the so-called ETs becomes clear. Like so many things, you only understand it when you know what you are looking for!

Over the centuries, the church, governments, kings and the elites have successfully kept the true situation obscured from the common man; they would not likely go along with the implications as to their received status and the way they are treated and regarded by the controlling forces. I am talking much deeper than political parties here; the powers behind the throne, not the public face that you perceive.

Be assured that after being privy to the 'inside track' for more than half-a-century, and now in my young 70s myself, I am not leading you down the garden path. I am sharing with you what you now need to know, for much of this will become evident over the next few years and you will be able to see what is actually going on in day-to-day events. Not, 'eyes wide shut', as is intended you should be.

Chapter 1: From Capital to Coastline

The concept of UFOs has captured the imagination of millions of people. The majority, according to a 2015 YouGov survey, no longer believe the phenomena to be a myth or an extension of science fiction. The question of unidentified aerial phenomena in our skies on a daily basis, has fired the curiosity of the human mind to enquire into the frontiers of all that which is unknown.

At the very least, the thousands of reports now accumulated worldwide cry out for rational explanation. Taken to its conclusion—the acceptance that intelligent life exists elsewhere—the answers would change the fundamental social, scientific and religious foundation upon which our society is built. This new reality would also bring great uncertainty about our place in the universe and the kind of relationship humans would have with others arriving from outside planet Earth.

We are already a race of space travellers; astronauts have travelled several times to our nearest satellite, the Moon. Sophisticated and intricate automatic devices, satellites and probes now litter the space around our planet and indeed the solar system in our immediate vicinity. We have been in the space age for over 61 years, since the launching of Sputnik in 1957.

After so many years we ask ourselves, surely we should have found obvious evidence of other forms of life by now? To which the answer may well be that we have, but we have not recognised it.

It is very easy for us to ignore observations that do not fit into our present concept of physics or the universe. For example, in olden days when people reported hot stones falling from the sky, no rational explanation could be found and it was dismissed by scientists of the day as impossible. However, as our understanding of astronomy increased and we came to understand meteors and meteorites, these former reports became acceptable to science and the 'impossible' was explained.

Against this background, the subject of UFOs, too, has emerged into respectability.

It is in this new atmosphere that contemporary reports can be examined without a large percentage of the information being lost, as has been the majority case over the last 60 years, since the term 'flying saucers' was coined according to the common description of the objects reported. How much precious and valuable data that has been summarily dismissed so far by the various authorities can only be guessed at. However, this mental block has now substantially shifted and we are capable of looking at this, the world's most baffling mystery, with fresh eyes.

Ufology has often been regarded as a cult. This may well be true, because study of the phenomena can often provoke a philosophical and sometimes even mystical consideration of who we are and where as a race we are going. Nevertheless, people's reactions to sightings do not affect the validity of the original reports. In my experience, the majority of observations come from very down-to-earth, rational people, consolidated in many cases by multiple witnesses and sometimes, even physical evidence.

A popular misconception is that people who report UFO sightings are in some way making money out of it. In all but a very few cases, it is quite the contrary; I know of many people who have suffered as a direct result, in some cases losing their jobs and even their friends. Reporting a UFO sighting has, in the past, brought their credibility and even their sanity into question.

This is just another illustration of our refusal to accept facts that lie outside our commonplace experience; an extension of the herd rejecting the black sheep because it might reduce or interfere with the strength and unity of the whole.

The incidents related in this book form part of a many-sided jigsaw puzzle. Superficially, they may appear to have no connection or relationship to each other, but deeper examination reveals a pattern, in fact several highly significant, somewhat disturbing patterns that combine to pose greater questions.

We are led to believe that all UFO activity is randomised, a scattered phenomenon not lending itself to rational interpretation. But might this simply be the result of inadequate information at our disposal?

During the 1970s, a period of intense aerial activity, reports and observations came in from all over the British Isles. 'UFOs Galore' made front page headlines in the Daily Express. A new wave of interest gripped the public as to what or who may occupy the space beyond our small world, highlighted by a series of new science fiction films.

The question is, will we have to wait until the end of the 21st Century to answer the ultimate question: Are we alone? Or indeed, have our cosmic cousins already arrived?

What, for instance, appeared in the sky over Wembley, Greater London, early in the morning of 15th November 1968? The witness, who wishes to remain anonymous, wrote to me:

> "About 1.20 am down the end of the Avenue over the railway machine shop I clearly saw the 'UFO'."

She included a detailed drawing, which showed a circular, disc-shaped saucer like a convex lens, green on the upper surface, dark red underneath, with a surround of port-like windows at its rim. It was ejecting jets of gas at its top and bottom axis. The witness continued:

> "It was below cloud level. I wasn't at all scared but my spaniel bolted indoors. I

called to my son and my husband to come out but was met by, 'Mum's up the creek' and other similar remarks.

"So no one else saw it but me, which often happens in these cases. I may add that I have seen lots of these unexplained objects. My next door neighbour has as well, so I don't think we are both stupid. They move in a wobbling fashion, often near the local flight paths. I have noticed that when an airliner approaches the light goes out suddenly as if they don't wish to be seen."

The following year, 1969, objects of all shapes and sizes were seen over the south of England.

On the Isle of Wight, Reg Hyde, who worked at Sandown Zoo, spotted 'a cigar-shaped object' at great height. "It was glistening in the sunlight," he said.

Police with dogs were called out to investigate a sighting made by a Sussex family. 21-year-old Paul Quick was pushing his broken down motorcycle back to his home in Storrington, when he saw what looked like a rugby ball in the sky. "It was one-and-a-half times the size of a double-decker bus," he said. He ran home and alerted his mother and two sisters, all of whom watched the object sitting on a crest of the Sussex Downs, about two miles from their house.

Near Beddingham, Sussex, farmer Ivor Main, aged 31, reported a long, thin, white-coloured object with two little tails. Meanwhile, in Surrey, Mrs Pauline

Cook called the police when something giving out a high-pitched whistle shot three times over her house in Blackdown.

At Folkestone, Kent, around midnight on 4th July 1970, Miss L. Couturier, Mr J. Male and Mr N. Ashman were out walking when they saw four green, heart-shaped objects surrounded by a distant aura. Visible for only a few seconds, they were heading from land to sea, north east to south west. The witnesses sat down to discuss what they could be and the aero forms reappeared in 'Y formation', going in the opposite direction. Making no sound they were quickly out of sight, heading north. Many people reported seeing the lights, sometimes changing from green to orange.

Also in 1970, the Ministry of Defence were reported as investigating a UFO report from Douglas Lockhart and his wife of Hackney, London. They saw a 'pulsating' flying object. It was yellow, black and red. Student, Philip Morris, claims he too saw a similar object over London's Hyde Park an hour earlier. It was changing from white to red.

Taxi driver, Stanley Simmonds and his wife, also spotted a silver object in the sky from their house at Clapton, London.

Kent seems to be a hotbed of saucer sightings as expressed in this letter from Mr Outram of Dartford:

> "One summer evening I saw what at first I took to be Venus. Then I realised the star was moving and increasing in brightness.

As it approached, it pulsated and its light changed from whitish to pale orange. It was a disc and emitted a pulsating sound. It stopped, then suddenly moved in the direction it came from. I have observed identical situations on several occasions."

From Chatham, Mrs E. Sage reports:

"People here have also had sightings of UFOs—only they are not prepared to let it be known for fear of being laughed at. I myself saw a flying saucer in 1969, you see we have what they call the Coney Banks here and below them there is this big field, so that really we are sort of in a valley. This day I saw the saucer hovering over the top of these banks. I was talking to two friends outside my house when I saw it. I said, 'Look at that saucer up there'. With that, as they turned to look; it seemed to disappear and they laughed and said I was going mad, but I know what I saw. There is a school at the top of these banks, which at the time, my son went to. When he came home I said to him, 'Did you see? …' and he cut me short. He said, 'I know what you're going to say. Did I see a saucer? Yes! We were out in the playground and it seemed to be hovering over the school.'

"By the way, this one looked as if it had a dome on the top. Then in September 1976, I was in a friend's house one door down from my house. We were talking, then suddenly she said, 'Here, look at that'. I looked and there it was again, then it just went as before. She said to me, 'I'm not even going to tell my boys, they'd think I was mad'.

"Two more people after this, who live in the same road as me, said to me, they were sitting one evening out in the garden at 11 p.m and saw this thing in the sky, flashing orange lights on and off. They said they knew it wasn't a plane as it moved too fast. The next day when our Evening Post was delivered, there were two teenage girls in it, who claimed they had seen this UFO the same time as the two neighbours.

"Three weeks after this sighting at 3:30 a.m. my husband was on night work. I was woken up by flashing lights out on the Banks. I sat up, and I might tell you I felt terrified, then there was this high pitched whistle that sounded like a jet when it starts up, then a sudden big whoosh. Then nothing; not even the sound of an engine of any kind. I wish I could have got out of bed, but I felt as if I had turned to stone. But that whistle sound was so bad I felt it go through my head; I had to sit there with my fingers in my ears, I couldn't go back to sleep. I lay there waiting for my husband to come in. Since then I have heard that reports were made to police that something had landed on the field.

"A couple of weeks ago we were getting a

lot of sightings at night. My own son came in one night and said he had seen blue flashing lights on something that was long, and it was just staying in the sky. Not moving. He was with a friend at the time. I have also seen a huge star with an orange light above it going at great speed across the sky. My husband is treating me to some naval binoculars as he knows I am interested."

Also from Kent, Mrs Lilley of New Romney writes:

"I have always been interested in UFOs, especially having seen one quite closely in September 1952. I was all alone at the time and I seemed to be transfixed. I lived at Sheerness then. It was hovering over the chimney pots and seemed huge, a round saucer shape with port holes. As I was watching, it started to glow and when it got very bright it disappeared very quickly.

"I have made a few other sightings, but not so close. One was Easter 1976, a cigar shape silhouetted against the setting sun. My husband was with me then. He was very sceptical until then. My son Colin, a policeman, has also seen UFOs"

The sound associated with some UFOs is recalled in a childhood experience of Miss D. Turner of London NW2:

"The recent publicity about UFOs has brought back a memory I have of when I was about six years old, about 11 years ago. I was playing by myself in the back garden. There had been two new shiny pipes put into the ground to hold up the washing line. I was playing by one of these pipes at the bottom of the garden and I heard a buzzing noise. I looked up and saw a long, silver object flying in the sky; it had a number of red flashing lights and was quite close to me. How close I could not say, but it got nearer and nearer. I knew full well it wasn't a plane flying so low, and besides it had no wings. By this time, I was petrified and I ran into the house crying. My Mum ran down to see what was wrong and I remember saying, 'Something came down from the sky, and it nearly touched my head,'

"My mother disbelieved me and I urged her to have a look, but of course it had gone. My Mum thought it was an imaginary game or something, but I knew it wasn't my imagination. I have kept this to myself for many years, apart from my Mum. But now I believe it was a UFO.'

At Elstree, Hertfordshire, a 16-year-old student of Aldenham School observed the inexplicable manoeuvres of another aerial unknown in early 1976. He recalls:

"It was during term time and our school is situated near Elstree Aerodrome. One evening, I was coming back to our house from the main school building across a field. It was a very clear night and I love looking at stars, especially shooting stars. I looked up and to my joy I saw a bright light moving, which I knew was not a plane from the airfield, they usually have a red light too. There was no noise and my joy turned to fear when to my surprise it stopped dead for about 10 seconds. Then it moved off slowly at a 90-degree angle from its previous path. It then disappeared behind our garage. I would say it was about 100-200-feet-high. I was so scared that I rushed inside and told my story, only to be laughed at by my friends. So no one else saw it."

In June the same year students were also among a group of eight people who observed a similar object over Eastbourne. Mr Fielder,.one of the witnesses, recalled that just before midnight:

"Strangely enough we were talking about outer space, because it was such a clear sky. We were all looking up into the sky when we saw a light above the trees in the garden. It appeared to be just an ordinary star, then it started to drop, as if it was a shooting star. We were all watching when quite suddenly it turned red. Not a brilliant red, but definitely red. By this time, our eyes were glued to the sky and we all rushed up to look through the window at the top of the house with binoculars.

"Upstairs we could see the thing more

clearly. It had stopped directly above Eastbourne College and was still red in colour. It must have stayed stationary for about three minutes, and as we watched it turned from red to white again. But this time a very intense white. It had an incredible luminosity and glowed above the college. It was like a theatre spotlight being directed on a certain part of the stage. Its brilliance was amazing. The strange and uncanny thing was that there was no noise whatsoever. At first we thought it might be a helicopter or aeroplane, but the night was soundless.

"As it was above the college, the thing seemed to increase its size by about three times. When we first saw it, it was about the size of Venus, gradually it started to move again and seemed to be coming straight towards us. It really was quite worrying. Then it just disappeared over the hills and we couldn't see it from the house or garden."

A UFO was also sighted by Mr Pestell at St Leonards-On-Sea in East Sussex. Later that year in October, Mr C. Foord of Wraysbury, Berkshire, witnessed the erratic acrobatics of aerial visitors. He was with his mother and remembers:

"We watched the object just hover for about three to four minutes. The object was just a white circle with a dull, white centre getting brighter to the edges. The object then

> started to move off in a zig-zagging movement, then stopped, hovered for a few seconds, reversed up and then shot of with the speed of a bullet in an easterly direction. Amazed as we were, about two minutes later another object appeared, same size and shape and followed the same flight path as the first. I couldn't explain this, maybe you might be able to match this with any other information you have been given."

Shortly afterwards, late in November a 'qualified observer' reported from Warlingham, Surrey:

> "An evening of no moon, broken cloud, about 10:30p.m. I went out into the garden. I glanced at the sky to observe Venus, large and bright with Jupiter laying low on the horizon in an easterly direction 'I have been interested in astronomy since a boy of 12 years of age. I am now 69 years old, and still very active and know the difference of what I see.

> "Into the heavens there appeared two red discs; not a brilliant red, more of a glow. They were about three inches in diameter, spaced about a foot apart apparently, travelling from south-south-west to north-north-east. The time of the sighting and leaving my vision was no more than nine to 10 seconds, disappearing over the rooftops at a reasonable speed. At what height, I am at a loss to say, it was a dark night, but I can say that they were below the cloud

ceiling. I live very close to Biggin Hill and Gatwick aerodromes, about four and 10 miles respectively, but I can say with absolute certainty that no aircraft of any kind was visible in the sky that night.

"The night was quiet, and to see two glowing discs moving across the heavens silently, no hum, no rushing sound as of wind, in complete silence, being held in a horizontal position, by what? Was there a solid body between them? Who knows? It has puzzled me much. One thing I am sorry about and that is, I have night glasses and a five-inch spectroscope but owing to it not being a good night for stargazing, they were not at hand. Who is ever prepared when strange things occur!

"Stars, galaxies, nebulae, meteors, these I can explain. What I have tried to describe I cannot explain. The number of known galaxies are many thousands and the stars contained in them billions upon billions. If only one star in these galaxies is a world like ours, then there are millions of worlds, larger, smaller, intelligent, some not so intelligent.

"If we are capable of sending a robot on a journey of many billions of miles or light years distant, to fall or orbit a planet of which nothing is known, some insignificant globe in a far-off galaxy, then reverse this theory. And why not?"

Why not indeed, Mr Eales?

Was it the same two UFOs seen over Warlingham which were also observed by Peter Seager from Dartford, Kent? He relates:

> "Towards the end of November 1976, I was looking out of my bedroom window as I always do for a few minutes every night, when two elliptical shapes flashed across the sky. They travelled just above the houses and flew exactly in a straight line and disappeared over the horizon in a few seconds."

The objects were also seen over Gravesend, Kent, on 30th November and later investigated by the Ministry of Defence who, however, failed to comment further.

Later from Bridgnorth, Shropshire, came the following report:

> "On 26th December 1976, I saw a red glow in the fields close to my home. It lasted about 10 minutes and then disappeared. This is the second time I have had such a sighting within 12 months.
>
> "On Wednesday 9th March 1977, on looking out of a window, I saw what appeared to be a bright-looking object in the same position as the other sighting. It was 8:15 p.m. It hurt my eyes to watch at first. My wife and I watched from a bedroom window. It moved very slowly across the sky before disappearing from

> sight at 9 p.m. We had opened the window but there was no aircraft noise at the time."

Essex was the scene of curious UFO activity, witnessed by the Draper family. On the evening of 18th October 1976, Mrs Irene Draper of Harlow recalls,

> "I don't want people to think I'm a nut. I actually saw this object and later there were up to five identical objects in the sky. Within a short time, there were three, hovering in a horizontal line to the left of Willowfield Tower. One suddenly broke formation and gradually accelerated until it was pacing an aircraft which was passing."

Together with her son, she continued watching and then without warning:

> "One of the objects did a strange thing. Mark had brought out a torch, which had a red flashing top. He turned this on and one of the five objects suddenly left its position and began to move closer towards us as if coming to have a look."

Her neighbour, Mrs Eileen Patience, was also watching by now and she saw the object swoop low over the area, examining the ground with a beam of white light projected from the underside. Were they ordinary aircraft? Mrs Draper was emphatic:

> "But as there was no sound at all, they could not have been aeroplanes. They were the wrong shape anyway, clearly disc shaped."

In January 1977, Mrs M. Kefford of Stratford, London, observed:

> "At about 3:45 p.m. in the afternoon, high in clear blue sky, two very large oblong-shaped objects lit from end-to-end, very brilliant lighting. They were moving, I think, in a westerly direction."

During the same period a green disc with two flashing lights was seen over Poole, Dorset, early in the evening. However, some people say UFO reports are just satellites burning up, as in this report from Chris Price of Ashford, Middlesex:

> "On the night of 7th February at 19:04 hours, my friend and I saw what appeared to be a star moving slowly across the sky. We first saw it passing the Pleiades and it travelled in a steady arc. After a couple of minutes, it changed course slightly, and then flared into a yellow light, then faded into a faint glow moving extremely slowly which vanished completely soon after."

But what strange device could fit the following description from Mr M. Malkin of Bognor Regis?

> "One night an object in the sky appeared from nowhere, travelled a short distance, stopped and completely changed a direction travelling at right angles to its original direction."

Or this next sighting from Mr P. Toms of Lancing, Sussex?

"The early hours of Sunday morning, 3rd July 1977 at 2:50 a.m., I was looking around the sky, which was clear. The brightest thing I could see was flashing red, which I thought to be Mars. Then after 10 minutes, I noticed another bright light. This one was a bit bigger than Mars. This light was almost overhead. It was stationary. After watching this for about 10 to 15 seconds, it started moving eastwards. I watched it for about 15 seconds, after that it got smaller and fainter and then it went out of sight altogether.

"One thing it did not have was a tail, also it was silent. I am convinced it was not an aeroplane or a helicopter. What man-made thing can stop in the sky and move off so fast at such a great altitude?"

Just two days later, Mrs Edith Just reported:

"During the night of 5/6th July 1977, I stayed with friends in Hastings. At about midnight, my friends woke me, and together we observed a hill just near us and over some trees, an unidentified flying object. It had the shape of a round, flat heater, the type that throws out air through the sides. On its otherwise flat top was a small structure, which looked like several cabin windows.

"The colour of the lower part of the 'spaceship' was a shiny orange and it appeared as though the interior of the top structure contained pink electric light. The spaceship moved slowly along to the other side of the tree and eventually disappeared behind it in total silence.

"During the following night I awoke from the noise of my friend's cat crash-landing in the same house at about 2 a.m., (was she frightened by any chance?).

"Due to the position of my bed, my eyes automatically looked out of the window in the same direction as the previous night, namely to the trees on top of the hill, where another flying saucer appeared, stationary and completely noiseless. This time I called my friends and together we watched. This object was oblong and pointed at both ends, flashing different colours into the surrounding darkness. At one end the colour was green and at the other end mauve. In the middle it was much brighter, rather like lightning. At times it turned, so that the underneath part could be seen, and at times the topside was visible. But it did not actually shift from the area."

Soon after, more reports came in which included this one from high over London:

"Last Friday, 8th July 1977, at around 2 p.m., I saw an object in the sky the like of which I have never seen before. It was high in the sky travelling from the north side of the Thames over the Shell building in the Strand towards the south side of the river, towards the Festival Hall. It was kind of 'V' shaped and as far as I could see grey in colour. I saw it for 50 seconds or so and then it vanished.

"I work in a 29-storey high-rise building on the eleventh floor and have good long-distance eyesight. We have a very good view from our office as a large part of the office is a huge glass window."

The London area also produced reports of strange objects with multiple flashing lights seen by police on six occasions during May and June 1978 over the Battersea and Clapham areas, and two reports of possible UFOs shadowing Concorde airliners.

The first was observed in August by Mrs Godden whose Chiswick flat looks out towards Heathrow. She stated, "A huge reddish ball appeared in the sky right in Concorde's path."

The second, in November, was seen by both airport staff and passengers at the Heathrow terminal. In transit, one traveller, Gerry Reeves of Harrow-on-the-Hill, said, "It could not have been an aircraft. It was too fast and too erratic."

Described as a 'triangular light', it was not picked up on radar, but was seen to hover for 20 minutes over the south perimeter of the airport, long enough for it to set off quite a scare, while attempts were made to identify the mysterious unknown.

Chapter 2: East Anglian Enigmas

East Anglia has yielded a rich crop of UFO sightings over the years. Of particular note have been those by qualified observers including coastguards and pilots. Some of the activity seems to have been centred around the US Air Force facilities at Lakenheath and Mildenhall. Of these, a number of sightings were confirmed by radar, which is a definite indication that the observations are not illusory. But the Anglian region has a long history of inexplicable happenings, as for example, remembered by Mr A. F. White:

> "My two sightings happened in Suffolk. I am a self-employed builder, aged 50, and have been interested in flying machines as long as I can remember. I have been a model aeroplane builder and flier, now flying radio control, for the past 30 years, so I think I have a pretty good knowledge of what I see with my own two eyes in the sky.
>
> "My interest in UFO's was aroused one summer evening 25 years ago, while I was standing on my doorstep enjoying the

setting-sun. I spotted a light travelling from the north to the west across the Suffolk sky over Ipswich. It was oval and going very fast, like a tracer shell, only bigger, and it went into the distance in about ten seconds flat without a sound.

"Again in 1952, I was plastering an empty house at Waldringfield in Suffolk, a very quiet village overlooking the river. At 11:30 a.m. I looked out over the river and to my amazement there was this huge dark round object like a dustbin lid just motionless in the sky. I turned my head away in disbelief. Still there! I watched it for a few more seconds perfectly still without a sound. Then I thought, 'Witnesses', and rushed next door to where my mates were working and fell over a heap of rubble, shouting to them as I rushed upstairs for them to look out of the window!

"You can imagine how I felt, all that shouting like someone demented, just to find a ring of smoke. I tried to explain to them that a few seconds ago there was this 'thing'. It might be of interest that just a few miles downriver at Bawdsey, is a radar station."

Mr White's dark circular disc was not dissimilar to an object photographed by 14-year-old Michael Albon over his house at Sudbury, Suffolk. He stated at the time:

> "I would not have seen the thing had it not been for my dog Trudy. It looked like a big ashtray upside down and the bottom was black and the sides a silver colour. Although the bottom was probably smooth, the sides of the object looked rough. It was silent and appeared to approach our house from the west and hovered around about 100 yards away and about the same distance from the ground. The distance is really a guess and it could have been any size because of the uncertain distance. After hovering around, it began to move away slowly and then went off quickly towards Great Cornard. It did not spin around but just floated.

The sighting was also confirmed by three other people, a next door neighbour, Michael's uncle and his father who said:

> "I have never seen anything like it before last week, but I do not disbelieve in them now, although I have not really got the foggiest idea what it was. It was certainly several feet across, possibly several yards."

In the neighbouring county of Essex, another youngster, Karen Wallace, aged 15, from Southend-on-Sea, was met with disbelief when she saw her UFO in 1969. She writes:

> "I know that people who say they have seen UFOs get laughed at. I found this out almost eight years ago when I sighted one. I

> was lying in bed one night and an object moving very fast flew by my window. I went to the window, and was just in time to see the object disappear across the rooftops. I went back to bed and a few moments later it went back past my room. I still have jokes directed at me. I did not report my sighting as I was not sure who to report it to, but I have no doubt in my mind that what I saw was not of this world."

Karen described the object as 50 feet in diameter, of grey metallic composition with multi-coloured pink, orange and yellow lights around The rim, a flashing red beacon on the top and a large, darker coloured square door on one side, visible as the object spun around like a spinning top.

Essex was also the scene of a sighting at 8:30 a.m., on 3rd February 1970, by Mr R. McCarthy, a passenger in a car travelling near Leytonstone. He saw, "Two cigars, one above the other, in the form of a cross. They were glowing red and visible for two minutes."

On the same afternoon, two pulsating bright yellow balls were seen at South Woodford by Mr D. Kemp and his daughter. They departed at high speed in different directions.

Some years later 13-year-old Jeffrey Browsdon reported:

> "In July 1976 I was camping with some Scouts at Thorrington, near Colchester. One night we were playing a game when

someone noticed a strange light. We all looked up and saw a light the size of an average star. It was moving quite quickly and it went up high and doubled back in an arc. Then it stayed still and it was joined by another and they were both flashing together. A few minutes later they both disappeared."

From Huntingdon, Cambridgeshire, comes this item from Mr W. F. Manley:

"I have seen one UFO. I am convinced was not terrestrial, it was of the conventional saucer shape with a centre dome which I observed for at least three minutes."

Also from Cambridge, comes a report of two stationary white lights over the city at 2:50 p.m. on 16th October 1976. After gently floating in the same place for three minutes they were suddenly seen by Mrs Kathy Tribe to take off in different directions at terrific speed.

Compare this report from Mr Robin White of Walton-on-Naze, Essex. He remembers the evening of 8th February 1977 at 9:50 p.m.:

"Something rather large, glowing, with a pearly white light went directly overhead and out to sea heading south to south-east.

"Feeling rather elated at perhaps having seen my first UFO, I walked on up towards where my wife and myself live. Still watching the sky, seven more objects passed over my head. These, too, glowed with a pearly, white light but their shapes were very distinct. These were shaped like flying wings or boomerangs and were heading in approximately the same direction as the first object and about two minutes behind, in wing formations.

"The outer two, each side, were also wavering and jerking in and out as if trying to join the formation.

"Three days later, between 5:35 p.m. and 5:40 p.m., having picked my wife up from work in Frinton-On-Sea, driving home along the seafront road between Frinton and Walton when we both saw a bright light, like a very bright star over Walton. The light was still very good and no stars were visible in the sky. Still watching the light, as we drove into Walton we saw people on the cliff top also watching, and to our surprise as the object came into view we noticed another light identical beside the first.

"The objects as seen from Frinton appeared to be over Walton but were actually further on, more towards or over the port of Felixstowe. As we watched, the objects, still side-by-side and definitely stationary, dimmed as one and just went out or disappeared as if somebody had turned a switch off. At the same time this happened we were stationary and watching with three other people who were as baffled as we were."

Mr White's UFOs are curiously similar in shape to an object report by Mr W. E. Pelling of Arundel who describes:

> "Just after 11 p.m. on a night in July, a luminous green object glided across the sky for about 15 seconds. Suddenly it changed course and was gone in a flash. It had no body and no tail, it was just a flying wing."

Later in February 1977, activity in the east moved to Lincolnshire. John Brealey, of St Hugh's School, Woodhall Spa, reports:

> "We went on to the school field on the 17th. Suddenly we saw an orange glow moving across the sky and over a wood called Ostlers Plantation. We were very scared. We had all got our compasses on us and they suddenly all pointed to the glow which was due south east. Then eventually it faded out and the compasses returned to north. The next night we went to the field again and as Edward Strange and myself went towards some tumbled-down pigsties I suddenly saw everything go red and we hurried back.
>
> "A year ago, my friend James Kirby saw a red glow over Bardney Wood. It rose, then went back down again. Other members of my dormitory have also seen flashing red and blue lights over the wood."

The same team of skywatchers were lucky again

and seem to have found a hotbed of UFO interest in the forest area near US Air Force and RAF facilities. They detail:

> "Last night, Monday, 14th March 1977, quite a lot of people saw a red disc going across the sky. I myself saw a deep red light, about 50-100 feet up, circling us. It was going over Ostlers Plantation, Bardney, a wood near our school, and made a circle right round the sky. This was about 7.20 p.m. Then at 7.50 p.m. I saw a red/orange light traveling quickly along the sky. Suddenly it disappeared. We are extremely interested in UFOs and have spent nearly £70 on a UFO project. Therefore, we would like to know what is happening, 'the coming invasion' or what?
>
> "Jonathan Salmon saw a very bright light through the curtains, then suddenly it vanished, also we have seen lots of lights over the school. Guy Anderson saw four Phantoms flying north-westerly, then a round object with a vapour trail crossed the Phantoms' vapour trail and headed on a westerly course. It was definitely not a plane. Guy states it was slightly larger than the Phantoms.
>
> "A few nights ago, James and I were looking out the window of his dormitory when we saw an extremely bright, red light shoot from east to west. When it had got about level with our window, it

disappeared. James saw the shape of a UFO, two saucers together with a dome on the top."

Mr T. A. Wortley of Norwich, recollects his experience of UFO interest in schools and children:

"I have been interested in UFOs since I was a child, when at school, aged about 10, we spotted a strange object over our school. Several years later, I read articles, and set about wondering about the incident. For 20 years I looked up in the sky, but never saw anything out of the way."

A UFO was reported as having touched down for a moment in a children's playground at Southend-on-Sea, Essex, at 8 p.m. on 11th April 1977. The incident was witnessed by an old age pensioner. On the 30th of the same month, a circular high speed object was observed at 4:49 p.m. over Ilford, heading south-west. It returned heading in the opposite direction, north-east, only 90 seconds later and was seen to have a central, fixed disc, surrounded by an adjoining one divided into quadrants, outside of which a spinning rim rotated faster than the eye could follow. The object was a metallic silver colour.

In May, schoolboys at Bransholme, Hull, saw a silent silver coned-shaped object and 24-hours later, Roy Thompson reported to police two 'flying saucers' over the River Trent at South Humberside. He spotted them from his caravan and described them as 20-feet long and spinning like tops. They were accompanied by a whirlwind noise which built up to 'a tremendous volume'. They flew north to south and were seen only 15 miles away from the previous day's sighting.

By July, the UFOs were back in Essex again. A lady golfer reported the following:

> "On Thursday, 7th July 1977 I was playing golf with a friend at the West Essex Golf Club. At about noon, we saw an unusual craft in the sky probably about half-a-mile away. It was a very large, cigar-shaped object; gun metal in colour, and when the sun caught it, a brilliant silver. It was very quiet where we were, and we were struck by the fact that there was no sound from it. We watched for about five minutes; it was travelling very slowly, and pretty low down and to my mind was piloted and not a balloon of any kind.
>
> "We eventually lost sight of it as it disappeared, climbing slightly behind some trees in the distance. While we were watching, two other lady golfers approached and also watched it with us. I am a sceptic on the subject of UFOs and am certain that you will be able to confirm that this was some kind of airship that was known to be in the area at the time."

The same lady continues:

> "On Friday, 8th July I saw an account by three schoolchildren that they had seen

something strange in the sky at about the same time on the Thursday, I rang the school this morning to confirm that this sighting was on the Thursday, the day wasn't mentioned in the paper, and to ask if since the report they had received any satisfactory explanation of the nature of the craft, but they have heard nothing."

Perhaps our witness, whose name I have not released, would be relieved to hear that she was not the only one to be reporting UFOs in the month of July over Essex.

Police Constable Peter Frost, aged 35, a dog handler based at Chelmsford, watched an unknown flying object for 25 minutes over Saffron Walden on the 18th. He radioed Stansted Airport, but nothing could be picked up on radar. The object was apparently cigar-shaped, hovered, flew in a circle to its starting position and hovered again at about 15,000 feet, then disappeared eastwards. P.C. Frost said it looked like a bright light, but there was no engine noise with it. The report was studied by the Civil Aviation Authority but remained 'unidentified'.

Ninety minutes later it showed up at Great Yeldham, the time 4 a.m., and was observed for 15 minutes hovering under cloud by a local woman.

The following afternoon it had apparently shifted its attentions to Chelmsford, where a 'cigar-shaped' object was over a park area. Together with another sighting over the site of a new prison at Stradishall by police constable, Trevor Gibbs, it brought the total UFO sightings in Essex to 43 in the first six months of 1977 alone.

One intriguing report, by the Ministry of Defence, involved an object seen over Cambridge Airport: "At 2:50 p.m. on 16th October 1977, an object was sighted coming from the south-west. It was thought at first to be an aircraft, but a radar control officer, who was on the runway at the time, thought that the object was too fast and was not on the usual approach lane. The object passed overhead and then returned, turned a half-circle, started to rotate and then left at high speed. It was estimated at a height of 15,000 ft."

The curious fact is that this sighting occurred exactly one year to the day and hour after Mrs Tribe's UFO sighting mentioned-earlier also over Cambridge.

The 'law of the odd', coincidence, or a programmed annual aerial surveillance? Mr John Willats, a Colchester man who has studied the Anglian reports, said of the UFOs, "One main flight route forms a direct line over the USAF and RAF bases in East Anglia."

1978 brought this fascinating experience from Mrs Waller at 10 p.m. on the night of August 27th over Pakefield, Suffolk:

> "The shooting stars caught our eyes first. There were three, all from the same area of the sky and all appeared to go down into the marshland between Kessingland and Southwold. A few moments after they went

to earth we saw a large star come from
where they went down and travel slowly
across the skyline, followed by a larger red
and orange glowing object, which was
followed by another large star. They
appeared to hover over the Kessingland
area and then moved very slowly out to sea.
They were evenly spaced and all of the
same height. We were sober and one of our
party was rather frightened."

On 28th September at 8:30 p.m., two Norwich schoolgirls observed several 'flashes' mistaken, at first, for lightning, which in their own words then, "Solidified and seemed to bank. Underneath it was red. It started to climb and then suddenly vanished." While visible the 'object' made a 'whining noise'.

Perhaps the most spectacular sighting of the region was made by two Cromer coastguards with the aid of high powered observation equipment. Seen on 1st January 1979 at 7 p.m., for a total of half-a-minute, they described the craft as:

"Some 200 yards long and throwing out
bright lights. At first it looked like a big
light and then an airship. It came just
opposite us about two or three miles out,
over the sea. It looked 200 yards long with
bands of whitish light coming off in all
directions. It looked like a spaceship."

The object, which had been previously reported travelling down the coast from Skegness was also seen by Mr Russell Dick and his family and confirmed by Gorleston coastguard who observed it travelling north to south and stated:

> "It had a line of red and green lights down the side and something like a bright glow surrounded it. It was between one and three miles from the coast and its height was estimated at 800 to 1,000 feet."

It was at first thought to be a Boeing 707 with all its lights on, but its speed ruled that out. The coastguard spokesman, in summing up, said:

> "We can only put it down as a report of something unidentified. We do not know the explanation, whether it was a space vehicle re-entering or what it was... We are left in the dark!"

Of course, the most important and startling series of incidents in East Anglian were the events of Rendlesham Forest in December of 1980. The incident is so well known and documented in the public domain I am only going to touch on it briefly here, but I will tell you the inside track on these events.

The first thing to state is it definitely did take place and all the smoke and mirrors in the world, including rubbish about lighthouses, will not change that fact. It was multiply-witnessed and documented by serving USAF personal and military police on guard over the few nights of the incidents and physical evidence was found on the ground at the sites of the landings. What they won't tell you in the public domain is the fir trees near those close encounters in the woods were covered in very fine and pure mildly radioactive iron dust. So much so that the army and Forestry Commission had to come in and cut them down, take them away and safety dispose of them; in other words, a nuclear clean up.

Where did the iron dust come from? Well, it was known from multiple similar events in the West and in Russia that UFOs, usually three in number, would come along to a nuclear warhead storage site—the Bentwaters Base was at that time the largest in Europe—and project some kind of penetrating anti-matter type beam into the bunkers which found the plutonium trigger material (the pits), extract it and convert it atomically to pure iron.

In some instances in the USA, uranium and some of the firing mechanism was also removed and this was then dumped at no great distance where it formed a very hot and temporarily radioactive heap for some days. In those cases, the pile was ceramic, green in colour and had pure iron nodules inside it, exactly spherical in shape.

I have examined this material and it also contained non-earth origin trace elements showing it had come in contact with some material from outer space. This was analysed under strict laboratory conditions and no mistakes were made in those tests.

Only after the fall of the old USSR, did NATO realise that it was a mutual nuclear warhead disarmament, being undertaken on both sides of the

Iron Curtain, by the UFOs.

When NATO leaders realised they only had largely blanks in its nuclear arsenal, all the witnesses were sat on and shut up from discussing this highly-classified information as if the 'enemy' knew, we could be toast. Of course the Russians were having the same experience and thoughts and kept mum on the situation too! This was one of the reasons that nukes had to be brought in to be serviced, re-armed and tested as no one knew which ones were live and which were duds.

Even now in 2018, under the current Trump administration, the plan is to make a lot more smaller and more 'tactical' nuclear warheads to re-equip the USA, as many of the current stock is also suspect. It had already been noticed with some concern that UFOs had visited minuteman silos in the States, shown they could both shut down the batteries of missiles and also, if need be, take over the command electronics and fire up the missiles to launch-ready condition. They were not fired off, but it was likely that they could also have been re-programmed and may go anywhere if the 'birds' were given flight. Any armourer will tell you that all ordinance has a limited success rate and not everything will go bang anyway, that is why there are so many unexploded bombs in the world.

So now you know why all the hoo-ha and character assassinations and baloney which was put out about Rendlesham and the nearby American-controlled, now decommissioned, bases. Of course, they hold nukes at the main USAF bases in Suffolk. It does not need more than two brain cells to work that one out. But there has always been a lot of UFO activity, surveillance associated with US bases worldwide, as the records show.

In concert with this unified 'smoke and mirrors' routine, the MOD and all other UK government departments go along with the, 'no threat to national security' mantra when any aerial activity is sighted in the vicinity of something sensitive.

While Russia used to paint old decommissioned cargo ships grey, place wooden guns on the deck and moor them in any available back estuary just to maintain an ever 'increasing naval presence,' so we also continue to build nuclear submarines and aircraft carriers (HMS Queen Elizabeth R08) which have out-of-date software and can be shut down by any close overflying Russian electronics anti-warfare aircraft. This has happened to a number of US Naval ships in the past couple of years. Why? Just to show they can. Bless!

It all keeps the armaments industry busy and gives people work, even if their efforts are almost completely pointless.

The cost of killing an enemy soldier in Vietnam was $29,600 and now one missile to drop on Syria is a cool $1.2M. Dumb bombs are cheaper, but less accurate. UFOs don't seem to bother to defuse regular ordinance although they have been known to switch off all the electronics on USAF fighter jets if they get too bothersome. They seem to know when the pilots are going to fire up the lock-on radars or arm their air-to-air weapons. Perhaps they are just reading their minds rather than listening to the electronics chatter, which is what the USAF Intelligence is downloading. They reckon that if any foreign fighter jet 'locks-on' and 'lights-up' a US warplane, it is already an act of war and they can immediately take offensive action. It happened to a couple of Libyan jets in the days of Gadhafi. USAF one, Gadhafi nil. Iranian airliners don't do so well either when the US Navy is feeling paranoid.

So you think we are building a good basis for interplanetary relations? However, it is a lot more complicated than that when you get beyond the regular military and into the 'special access programs'. Not even the US Presidents have automatic access to that. Those who had 'ET' briefings are as listed: Truman, Eisenhower, Carter, Reagan, Bush (elder), Hilary Clinton (Sec. of State) and off-the-record Trump. Putin is also fully-briefed and over in the UK former prime minister, Tony Blair was as well. Prince Phillip also requested a secure briefing and was given some very secure data. You will just have to take my word for it, but you will find it all checks out.

As Margaret Thatcher said on record, "You can't tell the people," referring to UFOs. How much did she know? We will see as we delve deeper into the dark side of history.

Chapter 3: Middle England and the North Sky

For some reason Scotland seems little favoured by the 'saucers'. Perhaps it is just the canny Scots keeping the information to themselves, or it may be a result of population distribution, but other researchers besides myself have noted a dearth of sightings from the extreme north of the UK.

I do have this one item however, from the west coast. My correspondent writes:

> "About 15 years ago (1962) we were camping near the Solway Firth and about 11:30 p.m. Sitting around the fire, there appeared a cigar-shaped UFO about 300 feet above us. It just stood still for about three minutes with a light under it and no noise. Then it moved off, still no noise. It was very big; we could not see the top of it because of the dark."

Another camping experience comes from Miss D. Stevens, of Nottingham, who writes:

> "I have seen something strange in the sky when camping in Derbyshire. I thought it

was the moon at first, but it sort of switched off like a light and I turned my head and saw the moon to my left. I went and told the others, but they weren't convinced. It moved very slowly and all the while it was in the sky there was a very quiet humming sound."

Also from the same county, Mr P. Sabine reports:

"I live on a high ridge in south Derbyshire. My wife and I were out walking towards the setting sun one evening in 1976 about August, when we observed what we thought was a star reasonably high from the horizon. But as we watched it changed shape, moved to another position and vanished. I don't think it was an aircraft, as I observe these every day from East Midlands Airport."

The Midlands have produced a rich crop of UFO reports over the years, as in this case from Mrs I. Burgoyne of Walsall:

"I saw my first "flying saucer" in the early 1960s in daylight around lunch time. It hovered just above roof level, was cigar-shaped and enormous, but the colour was indescribable, as it changed from blue, then yellow, all through the rainbow colours. The nearest one could say would be like mother-of-pearl, iridescent and changing as I looked. It was there for only a few moments and then suddenly shot away, so fast!"

The incredible speed of the unknowns is commented on in this report from Mr H. K. Mann of West Bromwich:

> "Five years ago (1972) the wife asked my son to fetch the mop in from the yard. He came running back in, very upset and excited, saying there was something in the sky that frightened him.
>
> "My wife and I dashed outside, in time to see a single object in the sky, very high up, and hovering. It then came much lower, moved to the left at a very fast speed. Stopped again and shot off to the right, at the same time climbing at a terrific speed."

Some time later, Mr Mann had another sighting, backed up by the co-witnesses of his wife, two brothers and sister. They jointly watched three huge 'saucer-shaped' objects covered in multi-coloured lights cross the sky in formation. He recalls:

> "These were most definitely not aircraft as the size was so huge. Once again the speed was great, and there was a humming top noise.
>
> "I can't remember the date of these sightings but I do remember the report in the local press the next evening, by many people claiming to have seen the same thing.
>
> "I can assure you this is completely true

and I consider myself a rational person. I have never seen anything since, but I am always on the look-out."

Another person keeping his eyes open is Mr C. T. Davis of Redditch:

"On two occasions when I was a caretaker, I saw what I can only explain as UFOs. The first was after Christmas 1973 when I was called out by some children to see some strange lights in the night sky. We watched these lights for about five minutes, first hovering then shooting off, disappearing behind a block of flats, then reappearing and coming back the same way. The police were informed by one of the children.

"Two days later, there was a small piece in the paper about the lights being an USAF experimental aircraft, but to see what those lights did would have put all our aircraft in the same class as the Wright Brothers' first aircraft!

"On the second occasion, I was on night patrol when I saw a light shooting across the sky. It went into the moon's glare where it stayed for at least 30 seconds. This really brought my attention to it; then another light came from a different direction. As this started to disappear, the first light shot out of the moon's glare and disappeared. I have no idea at what height these lights were, there was no noise."

One week after Mr Mann's sighting of his Christmas UFO, Michael Perking of Coseley, West Midlands, also witnessed the antics of a curious light in the sky. He details:

> "My father and I saw a possible unidentified flying object about three years ago on New Year's Day 1974 at around 12:30 a.m. The sky was perfectly clear, without any clouds at all,
>
> "I happened to go into the garden for a few moments and gazed up into the sky looking at the stars. Then I noticed after a few seconds that one was actually moving. It was exactly the same colour as the others, a light blue and twinkling. As I was watching it was moving upwards slowly, then downwards again. I hurried into my house to get my father to come out and take a look. Together we watched as the light was now moving left, right up and down in a square pattern. It moved away at about an angle of 35 degrees and suddenly vanished!
>
> "We calmly discussed the matter but came to no definite conclusion as to what it was, except it was no weather balloon or an aeroplane. Its manoeuvres were too tight in a short space to be anything we know of. Also there was no sound at all, not even any wind. It was a still night. I've often thought of reporting it, but about a year after the incident I read that in America the Air Force has a special department especially

for debunking any sightings."

Later in 1974, the month of March, Mr J. M. Lench notes:

> "One more report for your records: March 1974, over the M5 feeder road at Worcester. A saucer appeared, then slowed down, changed direction and accelerated away so fast" it disappeared within two seconds."

He described the saucer as metallic, silver-coloured and 70 feet in diameter. Also from Worcester, Martin Cooper recollects:

> "I am very interested in UFOs and I have read many books about them, because myself and my friend were only 11 when we saw our sightings. Everybody laughed at us. Our parents said it must have been something to do with the conditions, but we don't think so. Anyway, it was back in 1974 in early May at about 8:45 in the morning and we were on our way to school, when over the house we saw two white egg-shaped objects hovering. No noise, no pulsating lights, there they were suspended in space.
>
> "Suddenly they started moving parallel to us and then they accelerated away from us at a considerable velocity. It couldn't have been the conditions, because it was a warm clear cloudless spring morning. There were no aircraft around. Anyway, have you ever

seen an egg-shaped aircraft that can hover and then speed off at a tremendous rate?"

Throughout 1974 several sightings came in from Liverpool and in May 1975, a saucer was reported to have touched down for several minutes at Norris Green, a suburb of the city. Some witnesses thought they could see the occupants of the craft.

Further interest in motorways is recorded in this item from Risley, Warrington, in March 1977.

"When the weather is fine, I go for walks in the countryside where I live. This particular walk was alongside the fairway of our local golf course when suddenly I was confronted with one of these 'things'. I stood still for a few seconds and walked slowly towards it, when suddenly it flashed across the fields at terrific speed. I walked back for my stick, which I had dropped, picked it up and there was this 'thing' again! I stood for some minutes staring and trying to fathom what it was. It was similar shape to the 'usual description'.

"Was it a piece of farm machinery enveloped in ground mist? No! Was it a bunker covered with the mist? No! At this point, the sound of an engine starting up came from a vehicle that had been on the hard shoulder on the nearby M6 motorway. As the vehicle moved slowly away, the 'thing' shot away at terrific speed!"

Warrington seems a particularly favoured location

for the UFOs. Perhaps an interest in the British Nuclear Fuels plant there may be one reason.

Mrs Elaine Hazeldine has often seen them over the area. She writes:

> "In 1957, I was thirteen at the time, a group of us witnessed a 'disc' spinning across the sky. It was also reported by a man a couple of miles from the town. Nobody believed us! But it was reported in the following evening's newspaper. Also 18 months ago (August 1975), a picture of a disc was taken over the local power station."

She further reports an incident on 21 May 1977:

> "I saw this brightish object coming over; it was pretty high up. My husband and I both ran upstairs to get the binoculars. It seemed to hesitate a bit, then go further.
>
> "We then ran outside. By this time it had dropped considerably, it appeared just like a star. I ran to the bottom of the garden and shouted to my neighbour, who came dashing out with his binoculars and also his ten-year-old son with his telescope. This object then dropped down even further and passed over our houses. It was stationary for about three minutes and was so big and bright. My neighbours were excited; they had never seen anything like it. Then the object carried on along its way.'

UFOs were also seen over Warrington on November the 17th and 22nd, at 10:55 p.m. and 7:35

a.m. respectively. The first was reported as a 'lamp shade' with ports or windows, which entered a long grey 'cloud' and vanished. The second was a brightly lit cigar-shaped object that disappeared in the south east.

1977 was an exceptional year for UFO activity all over the United Kingdom. Particularly common were strange aerial lights that might easily have been mistaken for aircraft or satellites but for their uncharacteristic manoeuvres, witnessed, for instance, by Mr P. Stopher of Northampton:

> "On the night of 16th February 1977 at about 19.15h. I was driving home with my girlfriend when we noticed a star like object, about the same magnitude of Jupiter, where there shouldn't have been any star or planet. We pulled up and suddenly the object increased in brightness to approximately eight magnitude and then dimmed to its original brightness as it started moving. No noise was heard and the object did not appear to be moving very fast. We naturally assumed that it was a UFO and were wondering if you may have received any other reports of a similar nature around this time."

Try this one for size, Mr Stopher, reported by Mrs Patricia Hobson of Malvern:

> "When I saw it I thought, what a bright star shining in the daylight. Had it been dark, I probably would have thought it was another

star. But it was a bright light hanging downwards – about three times bigger than a star and about one tenth the size of the moon."

It was seen latter by licensee, Mrs Jean Hudson, who stated:

"It could easily have been mistaken for the North Star, except it was in the wrong place. It was obviously not a star, because when I looked again twenty minutes later, it had gone"

The 'star' was hovering over Malvern's top secret Royal Radar and Signals Establishment.

A spokesman for the Ministry of Defence said they would 'Look into the matter'. The sighting was later compounded by Mr Geoffrey Brown; who saw, a 'silver saucer shaped craft' over the same area. It was also seen by Jim Whitlock and other Lowesmoor residents, apparently moving swiftly on a flight path, between Kempsey and Kidderminster.

But at Ross-On-Wye eager spotters were disappointed when a large black cloud spouting flames which glowed in the night turned out to be only a hot air balloon piloted by two Mormons!

Worcestershire continued to produce reports including a, "saucer-shaped object low in the sky, from Mr John Simpson, to a 40-foot diameter glowing object carrying a red flashing light from Miss Jackie Hamblen of Malvern, and a mysterious oval shape spotted from Droitwich by Mrs Kaye Needham, who exclaimed:

> "It caught my eye immediately because it was so bright. It was definitely not a plane or a star because it was far too brilliant."

More reports flowed in from near Dudley, on the outskirts of Birmingham, Britain's second major city, where Mr and Mrs Jeffrey Watkins and twenty of their neighbours viewed an eerie visitor through powerful binoculars. Said Rosemary Watkins, who incidentally professes not to believe in UFOs:

> "It was a very bright white light surrounded by a red mist haze, and it hovered for a time. It definitely was not a star."

Meanwhile at Mons Hill School, caretaker Peter Hughes, together with his wife Verity and two evening institute students watched "an intense white light."

Mr Hughes, who called the local police, stated the UFO seemed to be at about 2,000 feet, and performed intricate manoeuvres at great speed. He said:

> "It was absolutely incredible. It was a very clear night and there was no noise at all. The light was so intense you couldn't distinguish a shape. It went much faster than an aircraft could and then stopped dead. It dropped, hovered and jigged about several times and then it was as though someone dimmed it out."

A Birmingham airport official stated that no aircraft had been in the area at the time.

This time in daylight and also from Dudley, Mrs I. Higson records:

> "While lying sunbathing in my back garden on Wednesday, 6th July 1977, I witnessed the following: The sky was bright blue, to the right of my vision was a large dense white cloud, while almost overhead was a small dense white cloud, separated from the larger one by a good stretch of blue. I saw something silver come hurtling through the sky and go into the small cloud. I watched and watched, but nothing came out of that cloud. A few minutes later the small cloud had completely disintegrated and vanished.
>
> "The only description I can give of the silver-coloured object was that it seemed to be like a miniature airship, cigar-shaped. The thing that imprints on my mind is first the speed the object moved, and secondly the complete disappearance once in the small cloud."

More UFO interest in schools was indicated by the landing of three circular objects in school playing fields at Coventry on 24th July 1977. They left oval impressions up to fourteen feet in diameter.

A much closer encounter was experienced by Steven Hutton of Droitwich; near the RAF facilities at Hartlebury. He and three friends were out for a ride on their mopeds when they saw two bright lights in the sky approaching them. One of his companions, Steven Clarke, takes up the story:

"The lights appeared to be about one-and-a-half miles away and at first we stopped to investigate. But then we realised it was a UFO and became very frightened. It scared all of us. We were too frightened to investigate. We started to ride off and a fierce gust of wind blew one friend off his moped and almost unseated another. The UFO, which had not made a sound, then vanished."

Steven Hutton, the unfortunate victim of the accident, was treated in hospital for an injured arm.

A similar encounter befell Andy McDonald of Runcorn, Cheshire, on 31st December 1978. He was riding his bicycle. when he heard a high-pitched hum and in his words:

"I looked up and there was a big white light with a very bright trail above me. It stayed with me for about ten seconds, then soared into the sky. I could feel it trying to lift me off the ground."

A Ministry of Defence spokesman stated of the New Year's Eve sightings, 'We have not been invaded. We think it is just some space debris burning up.'

The 'space junk' in question might well have been picked up by the installation at RAF Fylingdales, which looks out with over-the-horizon radars in Northern England, not a million miles from RAF Menwith Hill. Actually, the RAF logo is a bit of a joke, as it is a totally US installation, principally concerned with eavesdropping on worldwide communications, especially those in the USA that would be technically illegal to wire-tap without a court order. Along with the National Security Agency in Utah, the current practice is to intercept and record every single e-mail, electronic communication, telephone call, texts etc. allegedly to aid the agencies in combating crime and terrorism. That may be, but it coincidentally—or 'perhaps' intentionally—also allows complete surveillance of the resident population, 'the mob of Rome' that might one day wake up and riot.

Memories of the French revolution are still in the minds of those who walk the dark corridors of power, hanging on to their privileged positions.

What has this to do with UFOs? Simply that ET hangs around these listening stations in Utah, Yorkshire, Cyprus (the UK's Menwith Hill) and lets the electronic snoopers do a lot of the donkey work while just tapping into their systems and picking up the data for free. For details of one eavesdropping operation see my book, *The Welsh Triangle, Revisited* (2018).

Why would that be of interest to them? Because, like the Deep State intelligence agencies, they have a 'need to know'. Just like how the online retail giant, Amazon already knows what you are going to buy your kids for Christmas, has already placed the orders in China for them to be made and the search engines are already sending you headline adverts based on what you were searching yesterday. '*Minority Report*' is here now.

The 'ET' are heavily into quantum cyberspace, telepathy, mind control, self-preservation and colonial exploitation. That is why they came here in the first place. We were a green, undeveloped planet, easy pickings for the asking. In the old days, they needed slave labour to mine gold, which was easier to dig out than to make in a lab. They needed that to make monoatomic gold, a white ceramic powder for longevity and teleportation techniques of physical bodies; more on that later. They also needed water and biological enzymes for sustenance and amusement. They can get bored and have a wide range of emotions that need servicing, some good some bad, not all angels and not all devils either. Just read the ancient manuscripts, Sanskrit, the Bible – the 'gods' could be pretty extreme if they wished, for no humans much stood in their way—until now!

You also have the 'creators' who enjoy both making biospheres, civilisations, the art found in nature and also developing all of these for very aesthetic motivations. The good guys, if you wish, who set up a situation, a 'cosmic test tube', chuck in a bunch of ingredients and stand back and watch what comes out of it. A sort of cosmic *'Truman Show'*. These films often find origin deep in the human subconscious memory. We are daytime TV, a theatre, and as the Bard said, 'actors upon it'. Shades of *'The Matrix'*, but you don't need a plug socket in the back of your neck. It is all there built into the brain at birth.

From my study of the reports over the past half-century, certain patterns emerge. The UFOs respond very quickly to being observed by people. They come closer and interact. This may be from 'operators' on the craft who are telepathic, or it may be from the 'machine' itself as they are sentient. Even my car now thinks for itself, giving warnings of being too close to the car in front, so what would a machine be capable of that has been in development for several hundreds, maybe even thousands of years?

The 'machines', the UFOs, are also material 'printers' and can create physical things from a thought-form design, repair themselves and operate without operator instruction. Even US drones are now partially operated from internal coherent AI programs. The flight control of the Russian M29 used some eye movement detection systems on the 'heads up' to accelerate its pilot's speed to operate under combat conditions. Similar systems also are built into the stealth BI cockpit mechanisms along with their ionic EHT envelope, which not only causes them to be radar black but also moves the aircraft along faster by ion drive and reduced air resistance. You can see this sometimes on photos of the craft as a haze on the wings that is not just due to air pressure mist, when small contrails come off the wingtips.

ET craft have responded to being touched by humans, downloaded data streams, sometimes in digital format. They have interacted with the human brain and memory collection as at Rendlesham Forest. The messages are often cryptic, as for example the reference to 'High Brazil' just off Ireland to the west in the Atlantic. That was the Lat. Log. given.

Many of you receive whistles, hums and clicks in the ears; these are all telemetry used by the 'ET' systems for coms.

Chapter 4: The Warminster 'Thing'

Warminster is a small Wiltshire market town, which has acquired a reputation for supernatural manifestations on the grand scale. A place where the gods themselves are rumoured to motor around the heavens in their 'celestial chariots'.

During the mid 1960s, the area became famous for a series of persistently recurring strange events. These included local residents being woken in the early hours by curious and inexplicable sounds, some of which caused whole buildings to vibrate. Simultaneously, the skies over this quiet garrison town, bordering Salisbury Plain, seemed to be alive with UFOs.

Many residents dismissed the phenomena as the curious antics of the military, but it became obvious from the persistence of the detailed accounts that they could not be written off as man-made.

One strange luminous orb landed near Upton Scudamore, not far from the ancient Westbury White Horse. The terrified occupants of a nearby lonely farmhouse watched while a glowing, egg-shaped object sat only 300 yards away, emitting a barely perceptible low throb that made the whole house shudder.

Not daring to investigate until the light of morning, they found little sign of its landing place, but the ivy that had formerly covered the side wall facing where the UFO had touched down, had been shaken off completely and was now lying in a heap.

Here is another typical incident, this time involving a very down-to-earth Marine Commando, and what happened to his car at 1 a.m. on the August Bank Holiday 1974.

Stationed with his unit at Arbroath, 22-year-old Andrew Simpson was travelling near Lords Hill, three miles south of Warminster, having been driving for an hour en route to Devonport. Suddenly, he spotted that his car was being closely pursued by a bright-red globe of light, which appeared to rise from a nearby field.

It swept to windscreen height from ground level in a fraction of a second; then the sphere sped alongside his vehicle. Headlights paled and went out; side lamps followed, and the engine misfired badly. This continued for several seconds until the globe floated away. It vanished in a downward direction as if returning from whence it had come. The police later said he was extremely upset and shaken. "He was white-faced and blurted out his weird story excitedly and there was a deep sincerity in the way he told of a bizarre experience."

We have had a number of puzzling cases connected

with aerial sightings from military personnel and civilians over past years. Even Army officers report seeing 'spinning tops of fire' or 'weird light shapes in the sky' when 'things' fly over lonely roads and silent plains in the Warminster district. 'Monster glows' that sometimes swoop down to car level have worried motorists driving at night in past years.

Andrew Simpson is not the only member of H.M. Forces to have been confronted in such a dramatic fashion. Clive Brooke, a soldier from Sheffield, was quite calm when his motorcycle broke down in Warminster. He had heard of UFOs and had bought a copy of '*The Warminster Mystery*'. In the pursuit of his interest, a quiet walk took him to Cradle Hill on the night of 17th June 1976, arriving about 11 p.m. Walking alone in the still, quiet air, no misgivings or expectations troubled his logical mind. However, as he ascended from the white gate towards the copse on the hill, logic failed him as mind and hearing strove to understand a series of events that shook his usual iron nerve.

The warm, peaceful air seemed suddenly cooler; a breeze breathed on him, and the copse seemed to glow faintly. A mellow, modulated whine of 250 cycles per second, changing every second, came to his ears, together with a sporadic crack of high tension electricity. As Clive told me next day, "I know sound of a tank, being in the Army, and I am sure it was nothing like that. It sounded like the electrical works near where I used to live."

Then Clive thought he saw movement and a quiet,

unintelligible voice whispered behind him. That was enough! UFOs or no UFOs, the distant lights of the town looked far more inviting and Clive headed in their direction. "I can't be sure, but I would have sworn someone was following me," he said. "When I got down near the Army houses, I met a man walking his dog. I was very pleased to see someone."

Clive, having stayed overnight in Warminster, returned to the garage where he had pushed his motorcycle. Learning that they had not had time to attend to it, he kicked the starter pedal in the vain hope it would work. To his complete surprise it fired first time.

Having picked up his motorcycle, Clive looked again at Cradle Hill in the hot summer sun and returned home with memories he would ponder on for a long time.

Another case involving engine failure occurred one October evening. Ten friends were returning from a fishing trip at Portland, Dorset. They were travelling in separate cars, with the last in the convoy occupied by Mr L. Druce and his brother-in-law, Mr George, whom he was teaching to drive.

It was dusk as they passed through the village of Lytchett Minster, when Mr George spied an aero form hovering over St Peter's Finger garage. The car engine stalled. Mr George is quite sure he did not stall it, for he was cruising in top gear at the time. He drew his brother-in-law's attention to the object. Mr Druce estimated it to be about 200-feet up. It was cigar-shaped and some 70 feet long. He termed it coffee-brown in colour, with yellow lights of a rectangular shape along its length, giving the impression of observation windows. It was then that several other motorists stopped to gaze upwards. They watched the aero form for five minutes: then Mr Druce and his companion became rather scared, so got back in their car and drove on.

The object had risen higher in the sky and kept pace with them, crossing the highway en route. When they reached the Oasis Cafe further along the road, they again halted. The aerial unknown also stopped, hovering over police houses opposite the cafe. Mr Druce ran into one of them to enlist extra witnesses, but when he returned with a police officer the UFO had vanished.

He was on the point of assuring the constable that it had indeed been there, when it reappeared, this time in a totally different form, a blaze of coloured light. Red, green, yellow and blue bands of colour were clearly visible in the completely dark sky.

After a couple of minutes, the policeman went into the other house and emerged with a fellow officer. They kept their eyes glued to the spheroid of dancing colour for some minutes. Then the glowing object split into two sections; one went beneath the other, then re-joined it and took on a wholly different shape. After this manoeuvre, it disappeared fleetingly, then emerged again, brightly, for two minutes.

It began to move away, slowly at first, then

vanished very quickly as if tugged along at phenomenal speed by some unseen cable. The police officers sensibly took full statements and doubtless added their own impressions, but nothing further was heard of the matter.

During the sighting, Mr Druce experienced weakness in his legs and the hair on his arms stood on end. On their homeward journey Mr George suffered an unaccustomed bout of sickness. Since that evening he has also seen a large orange ball 'four times the size of a dinner plate' crossing the sky near Old Harry Rocks at Shidland, Dorset. One September evening he also noticed a stationary yellow 'scratch' in the sky, corresponding to an inch in width at arm's length and 18 inches long. Mr Druce, until then sceptical of all alleged UFO phenomena, now believes we are being visited by extra-terrestrial spaceships.

Mrs Dieterle of Bridgewater, writes of a near miss by another UFO on the A36 just outside Warminster:

> "My husband has also had an experience of a UFO. He was driving through Heytesbury just outside Warminster with a friend, when he nearly had a collision with a lorry whilst crossing the small railway bridge. It was caused by a very large, white, oval-shaped object suddenly appearing from his right and travelling slowly across his path. It went about 50 yards away and then disappeared. The only noise they heard was a slight whistling noise and at the same

time the car radio stopped.

"The passenger and the lorry driver all saw this happen and the incident resulted in a near-accident. All three of them went to the Red Lion and they were told by the barmaid that they were talking incomprehensibly. Obviously this could have been due to shock. This all happened in late 1972, possibly around October time."

Police and Army personnel are not the only 'qualified' people to have seen strange sights in the area which has affectionately become known as 'the Warminster Triangle', as evidenced by this letter from Dave Robinson of the University of Bristol:

"I have long been interested in UFOs and have read many books on these lines since I saw a UFO in broad daylight when I was a young child. Another boy was with me at the time, and we both saw it very clearly.

"We have made several sightings (with a different friend) on Clifton Downs in recent years both with the naked eye and with a low-powered telescope. These were very distant sightings but they weren't artificial satellites as they were able to stay quite still, and suddenly 'zoom' off at colossal speeds."

Dave Robinson's sightings are very similar to a report from Mr R. Griffey who also saw a curious 'star-like object' at 9:30 p.m. on 1st July 1968, travelling over Withywood, Bristol. He described it as taking a silent but zig-zag course over his house, suddenly stopping and hovering for two minutes, then continuing on its leisurely course.

A year later in the same area an object was seen at 11 a.m., this time in daylight. The witness reported it to be, "A big white disc, quite high in the sky, which stayed there for quite a while, but when a plane flew near, it suddenly went shooting off out of sight."

Compare the sightings mentioned in this letter from Bath:

> "You will probably remember when a flying saucer swooped over Swindon football ground in 1950. That same afternoon, I was out in the kitchen garden of Rode Manor and did not see or hear anything, but when I went back in the manor's kitchen, the head cook, Mrs A. M. Morgan, was highly excited, and said she had just seen a 'flying saucer'. It was flying very fast, and looked a bright silver colour.
>
> "Next day in the Sunday papers there was the story of the same flying saucer a few minutes after, swooping over the Swindon football field and many people saw it. The one that swept over the manor was going in that direction.
>
> "In 1954 Rode Manor was sold and we came to live at Woolverton (about half a mile from the manor) and I got a job as a baker's assistant and rounds man. One

bright morning about 11a.m. in March or April 1955, the van driver and myself had just pulled up at Woolverton, and a young lad came out to buy something from the van, when I happened to look towards the Red Lion Inn in a westerly direction.

"I noticed, flying from the south towards the north over Woolverton Woods, about a mile away, a big silver spinning object passing over the woods towards Bath. It appeared to be 100-200 feet across, spinning fairly rapidly and travelling some hundreds of miles per hour. Two fighter planes, looking like two grey mosquitoes were diving at it. It looked cigar-shaped but no windows or wheels, and no sound and dazzling as a looking glass.

"I drew the attention of the driver and the young lad to it and we watched it go out of sight. Then I asked them what they thought it was. One said it looked like a 'spinning disc' and the other said it looked like one of those things they called a 'flying saucer'. We had never seen anything like it before."

It was June 1976 when I, too, witnessed a UFO over the aerially haunted hills of Wiltshire. For some months I had been visiting the Warminster area and the night of June 3rd found my then-wife, Jane and I together with Fred, Paul and Shirley Burns of Lancing, Sussex, watching from Starr Hill, a popular venue for sky-watchers at that time.

Towards midnight, the moon having already set and the stars shining brightly, we suddenly noticed a curious phenomenon over the nearby ancient hill fort of Battlesbury. It was not exactly clear what its nature was, solid or almost gaseous, but it took the form of a torpedo shape with rounded ends, which we first perceived at around 1,500 feet in altitude, and probably in the region of 70-feet in length.

Its entire form was covered dull 'flames' of a deep crimson colour, which appeared to travel from the left end of the tube-like fuselage along to the right in continuous waves. Five to six waves were apparent at any one time and they appeared to traverse the length in two or three seconds, followed in the same frequency by further wave-forms. Their height was little more than the diameter of the 'Tube'.

For three minutes it hung silently in the sky, then swung slowly from a horizontal to a vertical position. The 'flames' paled and the vision was no longer in our sight. Whether the dark unlit tube remained or had now departed we could not see.

I recalled that Starr Hill had also been the scene of a previous sighting by myself and 30 other watchers a few months previously. The incident commenced as I drove in my Volkswagen up the dirt road leading to the barn that is the meeting place for watchers. My headlights caught their faces, turned as one to the northern hills where a dull phosphorescent orb was approaching.

Switching out my lights, I jumped from the car,

clutching whatever equipment came to hand and cursing that my camera was not yet loaded, since I had decided previously to wait and see which film speed would be suitable to the night.

I immediately judged that the object was already under a mile distant and approaching quickly. It appeared to be small in dimension, maybe only a couple of feet across its circular form. It was of low illumination by candle power and appeared like a large, dimmed mercury street lamp. Its speed was likely not more than 70 knots, and it descended in a gentle arc to the east, crossing our vision at a point some 300 feet distant when at its closest.

I had already given up on loading the camera in time for its overpass, but my electronic flashgun was fixed to the camera and my finger had instinctively shot to the 'on' button when dismounting from the car. As the unidentified light drew silently level with us, I fired off a heavy flash in its direction. The result was interesting. It made a sudden turn, instantly it seemed, downward and away from us, while simultaneously dimming out. Our phantom had disappeared!

However, another identical 'lit' as they have been nick named, appeared later that night. This came also from the north, passed east of us at a slightly further distance than the first, swung casually and in deafening silence to a point over a tumulus on Middle Hill, hovered and faded out.

This time I was not tempted to discharge the flashgun at it, fearful of scaring away our ghost and curious as to what it would do. That amounted in the end to very little, apart from raising a few 'oohs' and 'aahs' from the small crowd of UFO enthusiasts who watched the performance with a similar wonder to that of kids at a Guy Fawkes fireworks show.

Shortly after our June 3rd sighting, the Burns family and myself were the practitioners of a curious experiment involving one of the mysterious 'lits'. The experiment was to be taken dramatically further another evening, but on this first occasion its inception was almost by accident.

We had been watching for some time under a clear moonless sky, the evening broken only by the occasional sight of satellites orbiting in a stately fashion, following a regular arc until fading out as they entered the Earth's shadow.

Then we spied a 'lit', lower than the commonplace satellites, but still of low-powered magnitude. It approached in a straight line.

Somebody mentioned signalling to it and another suggested trying telepathy. Fred Burns switched on his cassette recorder to dictate the sighting. I concentrated on the approaching 'lit' and speaking quietly into the cassette microphone said, "Request you turn right by 90 degrees to the east."

It worked, suddenly making a sharp right angled turn without altering speed!

"Try it again," urged one of the party, and like a child excited with a new toy, but nervous of breaking it, we all concentrated on the light and gave simple single manoeuvre flight instructions. It worked again, and for the next few minutes the light and I played the game together.

However, on a request to 'come closer' it failed to respond and shortly afterwards, apparently having become bored with our inane and increasingly excited instructions, it resumed its former course and disappeared over the horizon.

A similar ability of the 'lits' to turn on a sixpence had been observed by John Rowston from Cradle Hill, Warminster on June 3rd, the time 1:20 a.m.

Previous inexplicable aerial manoeuvres of a similar nature are recorded in this account from Charles Bedwell of Cheltenham:

> "Having read about the many sightings of UFOs I should like to relate to you something that my wife drew my attention to one evening about 9 p.m. in later summer of 1973. It was already dark but very clear with the stars shining as my wife said to me, 'Whatever is that light up there?'

> "When I saw it, I thought for a moment it was a satellite far away to the south-west of us. In a matter of about three seconds it seemed to zoom to a position about overhead, at the same time growing a great deal larger, very brilliant and oscillating in a manner I have never seen with anything else. Then without turning, it started back in the direction it came from until it was just a minute speck once again, smaller in

appearance than any star.

"This happened half-a-dozen times before it finally disappeared from our sight, each time on exactly the same line of flight. First time I told my wife 'Perhaps it's a plane of some sort', but there was no audible sound at all and then I thought, perhaps it may be a helicopter, but again with no sound? With the speed it moved, I cannot imagine such a machine in existence at the present time. The height of this 'light' when it was overhead was about 20,000 feet as far as possible to judge and the light at this stage was bigger than any plane would give off and far more brilliant. Its actions I can only compare to that of an object being zoomed back and forth with a zoom lens."

The end of June 1976 produced the most dramatic rash of UFO sightings at Warminster. I recorded in my diary at the time,

"The night of 30 June was particularly rewarding. Present at Cradle Hill were Fred Hatcher, aviation engineer for BAC, author Arthur Shuttlewood, Barry Musselwhite, Sheila Meredith, Penny Stern, Jane, myself, Sheila and Helen. The evening was clear, no wind; the time 9:30 p.m. Fred had suggested that as there were nine people present, and Arthur added that it was the 30th of the sixth month, which adds to nine, we should try to send our thoughts out quietly and ask for some visual indication of the existence of flying saucers. It sounded a bit unlikely, but as we were all prepared to give it a go, we stood facing north and tried the telepathy routine.

"As we waited over the next hour, the conversation ran over other sightings and pet theories. Arthur and Jane, on top form with their continuous flow of puns and jokes, kept everyone amused and it was quite by surprise that around 10:30 p.m. someone shouted, 'What's that!'

Could it be that our experiment had worked, for gliding in from the north at an altitude no higher than 8,000 feet (Fred estimated) was a circular craft carrying clearly seen lights. Its speed was quite slow, (estimated 200/350 knots) and it undulated slightly in its flight path. No flashing anti-collision lights could be detected but through 10x50 glasses five white lights could be seen arranged in a square on the underside, the fifth being in the centre. Also, a red light ahead and below the central light. All lights were pin-point and constant. Having myself seen many military aircraft over Salisbury Plain, I was certain it was not of MOD origin. Its body was metal grey, visible in the fading light. No sound could be heard and as it flew over the copse at Cradle Hill, some quarter mile away, and banked to the west, it clearly had no wings but was just a body in flight. No windows could be observed and no exhaust. A very, faint sound like that of a turbine was detected by some watchers, not others, but it in no way sounded like a jet or a turbo-prop engine.

"Later in the evening, we returned to our base and sat chatting in the paddock under a star-spangled sky. The occasional satellite passed over. Then, without warning from a part of the heavens where no other object could be seen, several bright pin-point flashes blinked. They were very bright and of a high colour temperature, towards 5000 degrees kelvin. One had the impression that a directional flash gun was being used as the flashes were all of very short duration, maybe 1/1000 sec. No aircraft noise could be heard at the time or afterwards.

"Whatever was making the flashes was high in the sky, but much lower than an orbital object for the beam of the light could be seen in the air flaring downwards for a short distance from its source which was standing still. Barry flashed three, plus three, plus three, dots with his powerful torch and at once the signal was returned. The quickness of the response gave the impression that the process was automatic rather than manual. I have noticed this feature before and it would seem that any short sequence is faithfully returned immediately. The flashes were definitely not lightning as they were from a point; anyway, there was no cloud. The chances of them being meteors was also dismissed as they all occurred at the same point. High flying aircraft don't stand still, so that was out, too.

"Having retired to the top of the house, Fred observed the lowest of the UFOs that week. While lying on his bed overlooking Elm Hill, he saw a golden disc glide in from the west and dip towards the golf course, then depart eastward. The time was 4 a.m. and the same thing happened again about 4:10 a.m., but this time going east to west."

Many people come to Warminster and see only 'satellites'. However, if these objects do not stop, change direction, or signal one cannot say if they are man-made or not. The only point I would like to make is that many of these lights that travel over are very bright, as bright as Venus or the Echo type satellite. They also quite often transit in a level path rather than a curve. Their direction has no relation to that of the wind and they often switch on or off before they reach any occulting obstructions such as clouds or hills or ground haze. Some nights, one can go out and see, given a clear sky, a few satellites pass over. Other nights the numbers seem quite out of proportion.

I have had observers come back after a three-hour watch and declare that they have seen no UFOs but recorded 38 satellites, all of them nearly overhead?

Some people watching come armed with 'UFO detectors', a primitive device using a compass needle to detect magnetic variation. On 10th July 1976, a report from Robert Norman and Kevin Goodman gave some indication that they may work. At 11:29 p.m. two detectors sited at Cradle Hill, away from cars and watchers and protected from the wind, went off together for no apparent reason. Some 15 seconds later, a UFO was seen going over. It pulsated and then went out, flashed once brightly as if in farewell and was not seen again.

Since the commencement of my research, I have been receiving letters daily from people who have seen UFOs, pilots, engineers, vicars among them. Three or more a week come in from the Warminster area, and that's after I've written off space junk, meteors and such like. I don't ask you to believe it; go out and look for them, then you can judge for yourself!

I have often thought of Warminster as a kind of celestial 'Spaghetti Junction', (the tangled junctions of motorways near Birmingham). You can watch a UFO arrive, then go off in another direction, as if routes converge there.

Certainly, the county of Wiltshire is one of the most aerially-haunted in the country; enough to attract people from such far-off lands as Canada, Australia and America to come and watch from the hills.

Sometimes UFOs are seen low down, as in the instance of 'a great yellow glowing sphere' seen in 1974 over treetops only 60-feet-high. At first it was mistaken for the moon by a farmer at Chapmanslade, near another mysterious vast hill earthwork and 'fort' known as Cley Hill, said to be the site of magical ceremonies in the Middle Ages, and even to this day.

It was from Cley Hill that a London air charter operator sighted 25 curious lights or 'lits' in a single evening, transiting the sky on 8th July 1976, including one very bright yellow 'flare-like orb', which crossed from horizon to horizon in under a minute at 4 a.m.

The density of sightings of the uncanny moving star-like 'lits' objects over Warminster, is certainly worthy of mention. Take this example from the skywatch log of 30th and 31st July 1976:

Time 30.7.76	Appeared	Departed	Transit Time
10:30 p.m	Overhead	ENE	Very short
10:41 p.m	Overhead	E	Very short
10:46 p.m	Overhead	ESE	Very short
10:48 p.m	S	ENE	Very Short
11:11 p.m	NW	S	1 minute
11:59 p.m.	W	SSW	1 minute
12:18 a.m.	E	S	30 Secs
12:47 p.m	S	N	1 min
12:56 a.m.	NW	SSW	3 minutes

31.07.76

1:05 a.m.	SE	NE	30 seconds
1:14 a.m.	NE	Overhead	30 seconds
1:14:30 a.m.	Overhead	NE	30 seconds

The evening of 31.07.76

10:18 p.m	N	ESE	2 minutes
10:21 p.m	SSW	NE	4 minutes
10:55 p.m	S	E	2 minutes
11:01 p.m	Overhead	Overhead	30 seconds
11:05 p.m	Overhead	N	Very short
11:20 p.m.	Overhead	E	1 minute
11:30 p.m	SW	S	1 minute
12:00 p.m	Overhead	N	1 minute

Also witness to the events of 30th July was Maureen Rowston who, at 1:21 a.m., saw another UFO to the north-west, weaving about and with a 'bow-wave'. The sky was clear with no moon and she watched the 'lit' for ten seconds before it disappeared.

Maureen, who has strong views on UFOs, stated at the time:

> "This one was lovely. A big bright orange thing, it moved in jerks, as if it was making observations. I believe it was operated by beings vastly superior to us. We're making enough nuclear bombs to blow ourselves up a thousand times. I think they're trying to warn us, before it's too late."

29-year-old Maureen, who admits to having watched the skies for 12 years before her first sighting at Warminster, where she saw five in one evening, went on:

> "When you think that nearly every star is a sun like ours, with millions of planets like our world spinning around them, it's unthinkable that life could exist on just one planet. It would be ridiculously vain to think our earth is unique. And if we can send satellites to Mars, doesn't it stand to reason that there must be more advanced planets capable of sending machines to watch us?"

Would it be facetious of me to note the nearby location of the military and research facilities at Porton Down, a little east of Warminster? Wouldn't the supposed 'alien beings' have cause to keep a watchful eye on them?

A little after the sky activity of June and July, Mrs P. Manners wrote to me about her family's sightings:

> "One night last summer (1976) around dusk, I happened to go to the back door, and on looking up, saw two bright orange balls of light travelling one behind the other across the sky. To my eye, they were each about the size of an old style penny held at arm's length. I know I didn't imagine it, because I looked back into the kitchen to call my husband, and when I looked again

they were still there, but the third time I looked they had somehow disappeared.

"Also my young daughter, then nine years old, was playing in the field near our house with a friend when, she says, an orange object, as large as the moon, flashed across the sky and stopped. It was orange in colour, round in shape and had white lights flashing about one-third the way down and red lights flashing near the bottom of the object. It made no sound, and after disappearing once, reappeared again then flashed away out of view. I've questioned her several times since and her story is always the same."

A near identical report was later filed by Mr D. Howaitt, of Salisbury, Wiltshire's county town, famous for its cathedral spire. He wrote:

"Early one Saturday morning at 4:30 a.m. in September 1976, my mate and myself saw an orange object about the size of a football. We watched it for about three to four minutes and then it seemed to gather speed and faded out. It came from the north and went to the south.

"As I am a night patrolman, I have seen quite a few of these. Another one was on 29th January 1977, while on patrol at about 11:30 p.m. My mate and myself saw two orange objects going from north-west to south. They were about the size of footballs in the sky. There was about 50 to 60 feet between them. Then a little way behind them there was a smaller one, it seemed to have a white and orange flashing light. They made no sound at all."

Previously, on 16th October 1976 at about 11 a.m., a Warminster youth and two of his friends were travelling in a small van towards Bath. They were just outside the city boundary when Steve noticed, looking out of the window, what he described as 'two metallic looking spherical objects'.

The van was going at about 40 to 60 kilometres per hour. The objects were hovering over a small village in a valley and to the observers appeared to be about three degrees elevation from the line of the road. They seemed to have no relative motion. Steve then called the attention of his two companions who agreed that the objects could not be natural or man-made objects.

The van then went round a bend and behind a bank of trees and so the objects disappeared from their sight. When they emerged from behind the trees they saw only one object. From this they could not define whether it was one of the original ones, or quite separate. This appeared to be at an elevation of about five degrees higher than the original sighting. The van then went round another bend and by this time the objects had disappeared.

On 22nd November at 7:35 p.m., a 150-foot diameter yellow glowing object was sighted travelling at high speed and soundlessly over

Warminster at 2,000 feet. It turned in a north-easterly direction and appeared to be spinning.

Previously on 23rd October, a white ball-like orb was seen to fall to earth over the copse at Cradle Hill, overlooking the town, by a Mr Nickells. The phenomena was accompanied by some flashes and some shooting stars. The possibility of a meteor or even ball lightning cannot be ruled out in this particular case.

But what explanation would fit this report from Chris Butler?

> "On 2nd January 1977, I saw a bright orange, cigar-shaped object with rounded ends. It made no sound as it moved north over the golf clubhouse at Warminster. Its size was about a half-inch diameter at arm's length and after looking at it through 8x30 binoculars, I could see it had a grey patch in the middle. The time was 4:19 a.m. and it was visible for two minutes."

Four days later, a similar object was seen, travelling south-east only a, couple of hundred feet off the ground at 6:02 p.m. It disappeared into fog over the 'hill fort' at Battlesbury.

Reports continued to flow in from Warminster throughout 1977. I myself saw a bright orange ball travelling silently and at low altitude in an undulating movement from horizon to horizon. I was accompanied at the time by journalist Tony Gray who, though originally sceptical of UFOs, admitted that he could find no ready explanation for the object we observed.

On 10th August at 10:50 p.m., three dome-shaped 'saucers' were sighted over the town and confirmed by an independent witness. They hovered, then shot off at terrific speed. On 27th October, at 6:18 a.m., two patrolling Salisbury police constables also reported UFOs over the now famous 'Warminster Triangle' as the press had dubbed it.

However, perhaps the most intriguing happenings at Warminster have been the landings of strange craft, sometimes even leaving physical evidence, allowing examination of the marks after the event. Even back in 1967, the Army bomb disposal unit had investigated a mysterious crater at Charlton, Dorset, for which no explanation could be found.

On 12th December 1970, other curious marks appeared overnight in Kent and at Blandford Forum, Dorset. In some cases, areas of soil and vegetation had been removed and was never found, although an extensive search was made of the sites.

On the evening of 26th August 1972, American journalist, Bryce Bond, was among witnesses who experienced the ascent of two UFOs from Salisbury Plain. Curious flattened landing marks were found in the cornfields afterwards, all showing a counter-clockwise motion of the force that had caused them.

During 1975 to 1977 a series of UFO landings occurred resulting in the evidence of a number of 'UFO nests' and a close encounter ending in a chase by two researchers. However, the supposed 'Ufonaut' mysteriously vanished, as described by

Steve Evans writing of his and his friend Roy's unnerving experience of 5th October 1975:

> "We returned to Heaven's Gate at 7:15 a.m. As we walked in the direction of Longleat House, Roy became increasingly unnerved until, as we walked across the flat-topped hill overlooking Longleat, we both felt that we were being watched. As we were returning to the car at 7:30 a.m., I glanced towards a clump of bushes through which I could distinctly see a figure turning away from us. He then started to run away and some impulse made me chase after him. We also noticed that we were running over twigs and bracken, though I am certain that his feet were making no noise.
>
> "He ran towards what turned out to be a hollow bush and as he ran through a kind of rounded entrance, he slowed and looked back at us. After a second or two, he turned and ran into the bush. We followed, 15 or 20 seconds behind. I was the first to arrive at the bush and on doing so, found it to be empty. I also noticed that it had turned very cold. Roy arrived a few seconds later and as he came through the entrance, he stopped for a split second and we thought—both of us had the impression—that someone or something had brushed past him and out into the open."

Steve Evans was also witness to a sighting the following year when he reported:

"The location was on a small track just to the left of the Bustard Hotel about a mile north-east of Shrewton. It was the late May or August Bank Holiday of 1976, at approximately 4 a.m. The witnesses were Syd Hutchinson of Southampton, and two others whose names I do not have. At about 4 a.m., a horizontal formation of six orange lights fell slowly to the ground. After a few minutes, a red light shot vertically into the air from the right end of the formation. After a short while this was repeated, but with a green light from the left end. After 20 minutes, the lights rose high into air and faded from view. A triangulation was taken at the time of the sighting and as soon as it got light enough Syd and another of the witnesses drove to the spot, but were warned off by an Army sign."

The description could be explained as military parachute flares, but Shrewton was also the location of a multiple sighting by the Rattigan family and some friends on 24th July 1977. All seven witnesses drew independent drawings of a dark, disc-shaped 'flying saucer' surrounded by a sort of halo. Mr Pat Rattigan, a Post Office technician and a very down to earth person, commented on his family's sighting:

"In my honest opinion, this was the real thing. The children drew these pictures in my kitchen separately from myself and the others."

Another resident of Shrewton thought he had seen one of the 'discs' land near Salisbury Plain one week previously. However, the experiences of Roy Fisher from London, open up even wilder aspects of the phenomena at Warminster. He states:

> "I am writing of a 26th/27th June 1976 sighting at Warminster; I will not list the sightings we all saw from 11:16 p.m. to 1:10 a.m. at Starr Hill that night, as you know as well as I what we all saw. I hope you remember me, I was talking to you most of the night with my friend Steve Evans. Just after you departed, Steve and myself went back to Cradle Hill where I joined a few other people sky-watching. Our first sighting was just after 1:10 a.m., which was a brilliant white light which shot straight down from the sky over the copse area.
>
> "We were all talking about the light we had just seen, when someone flashed their torch over the field towards the golf clubhouse. Then a great crackling sound came straight at us! We all jumped back! The sound came to where I was standing and then swung round to the rear of the party. The sheep in the next field went mad. There was no visible thing to be seen. In the morning, I saw the grass was flattened in a funny way. I have enclosed a picture of this taken with my Polaroid Land Camera Swinger II.
>
> "Witnesses present were Steve Evans,

myself, Terry and Bridget Chivers, P. Pegler, Peter and Paul Humphreys, all from Melksham. At 1:30 a.m. a very bright light crossed the sky over Cradle. At 1:40 a.m., a loud clicking sound to the right of the copse. 1:50 a.m., white light zig-zagged from south to north above Cradle. 2:20 a.m., white light zig-zagged and circled south of Cradle, disappeared at 2:22 a.m. 2:55 a.m., white light zig-zagged south to west. 3:20 a.m., white light crossed west to east. All present saw these unusual lights.

"When the other people departed early in the morning, Steve and I went to Heaven's Gate. It was very bright, no other people were about, when I heard heavy footsteps in the bushes, which are very thick for people or animals to walk through. The footsteps were very heavy and loud and they were coming in our direction.

"I called out, and the footsteps stopped, then came harder and louder. I called out, 'Who's that?' and the footsteps came on still, then they stopped. We stood there for about 10 minutes, but nothing else happened. We looked through the bushes which were very thick, but no marks were found. We only hoped that some other people could have been there but it was early in the morning, about 7:30 a.m."

Unfortunately by the summer of 1977, the work of the various research groups operating at Warminster had become known outside of that circle. A curious campaign of intrigue and controversy seems to have been mounted against continuing their experiments. Amidst this controversy and the resulting internal conflict between individual research groups, the investigations at Warminster were eventually abandoned, or at least indefinitely postponed.

However, the question arises, do we follow the cautious thinking of some, that in a universe of potentially superior intelligences it is best to be left alone, or should we pursue the curiosity that burns in us and try to solve the UFO mystery?

Chapter 5: Hampshire Happenings

The UFO mystery deepened in a dramatic manner just before Christmas 1976, when a startling contact occurred on a lonely road outside Winchester. The report was confirmed by independent witnesses and ground marks, found later by researchers. But before we cover this story in detail it is important to mention here that the scene of the events lies on a well-established route used by UFOs over the New Forest and the Isle of Wight.

Even back in 1971, reports were flooding in of strange craft flying on this invisible road in the sky.

On Saturday 13th March 1971, a very large luminous object was seen in the east, from Bursledon Bridge, near Southampton. Orange in colour and stationary in the sky for approximately two minutes, it then moved very slowly first towards the south and then disappeared above cloud level over Wiltshire. Nine days later, this enquiry came from a Portsmouth resident:

> "I should be interested to know whether anyone saw a strange object in the sky on the evening of 22nd March about 8.15 p.m. It was seen by my daughter and her young

man as they were travelling by car. This
object was like a flying saucer with flashing
red lights and it remained in view all the
way from Fareham until they reached
Cosham."

Soon afterwards, on 1st April at 9:30 p.m., a mystery object was seen in the sky at Hungerford, near Southampton. The object was travelling from north-east to south-west, orange in colour and about the size of a pea held at arm's length and on 13th April, another object was seen over Titchfield from Fareham, Hampshire. The time was 10:45 p.m. and the UFO was traveling from north-west to south, again, orangey red in colour. It was in sight for about one minute.

However, the night of 10th July 1975, produced this curiosity from Gus and Muriel Langdon of Shanklin:

> "It was a vivid green and seemed to curve in the direction of Sandown Airport. The time was 1:30 a.m."

Mrs Langdon added:

> "Now we are wondering whether anyone else saw the object. I suppose we are going to have our leg pulled about flying saucers, but we certainly would like to know what the mystery object was. I think quite a few people must see this sort of thing, but don't like coming forward in case people might make fun of them."

About the same period, Mr Thomas Reynolds of

Adgestone saw an immense lighted object 150 feet above his farm as he was preparing to milk his cows at 6:30 a.m. The 70-year- old farmer vividly recalls:

> "It didn't make a sound, I couldn't see the shape, it was just a bright light about a 100 feet in length by 30 feet wide. It was a bit frightening. The object was travelling very slowly, about 30 mph. It was an experience I shall never forget. The object disappeared towards Brading Down."

1976 and 1977 were bonanza years for UFO reports in the Hampshire/Solent area, in common with a tremendous upturn in sightings nationwide.

A particularly detailed observation came from David Spicer, a television engineer and former serviceman in the Royal Navy aboard the aircraft carrier Hermes. He described in April of 1976 at 10:30 p.m. a peculiar bright light, 2,000 feet over Ryde Airport:

> "The light was motionless for four or five minutes and then suddenly shot straight upwards at an alarming rate."

Mr Spicer watched the light with his wife. Together they saw it move to one side and then towards them at high speed until it was overhead, when it stopped dead. It now appeared to be a spherical black mass with red lights on the perimeter half-way up. David further commented:

> "I've never seen anything like this. It was too low for a star and too bright for an aircraft. Its vertical speed was amazing".

Mr Rodney Riddell also spotted a strange craft in the sky from nearly the same location earlier in the year. His sighting was later confirmed by a meteorological officer at Portsmouth and was the subject of an unpublished Ministry of Defence inquiry.

Events intensified with an incident at Newport, Isle of Wight, in September. Mrs Shirley Rimmer, a nurse, was among several people terrified by two large white discs, which appeared over the Pan estate and then zoomed off at high speed with a sound like thunder accompanied by the noise of ringing bells. Mrs Rimmer said:

> "The houses trembled and I remember thinking, "I hope it's not one of those earthquakes that have been happening around the world"

Mr Tim Woodward, another witness, said the bang shook his house. On rushing outside he saw the discs, part of a formation of five, moving away at 'terrific speed'. Oval and silver-grey in colour, they departed, stopping only momentarily over Godshill, where they hovered before travelling out of sight.

They were also seen by 17-year-old Andrew Gordon from Niton, who said the noise was so loud, "At first, I thought it was warships firing their guns."

The evening of 14th November 1976, was the commencement of a classic, long and complicated contact story involving the principal witness of Mrs Joyce Bowles and some of her friends.

The scenario subsequently became known as 'The Winchester Mystery' and started as Mrs Bowles, accompanied by a close family friend Edwin (Ted) Pratt, was driving from Winchester to Chilcomb at around 8:50 p.m. in Mrs Bowles' Mini Clubman.

While travelling on the A272, their attention was caught by an orange glow in the sky. Shortly after this they turned off the major road into Chilcomb Road, a narrow lane with wide grass verges. It was at this point that, according to the witnesses, the Mini, although only travelling at 25 mph, began to, "Shudder and shake as though it were coming to pieces,"

Mrs Bowles, who was driving, found that the vehicle was now out of her control and despite her wrestling with the steering wheel and taking her feet off the accelerator, the car seemed to be slightly lifted. It moved sideways on to the verge, straightened itself and after a few yards was brought to a cushioned stop by what appeared to be some sort of 'invisible barrier'. Throughout these alarming moments, Mr Pratt had also grabbed the wheel, but to no effect, and the engine ignition had been turned off, before which, the Mini was revving as if the throttle had jammed.

Mrs Bowles states:

> "That is when we saw, what I shall say, a cigar-shaped object, hovering in front of us. Inside were three figures."

The object was hovering just over a foot off the ground, was 16-feet-long, with a forward cockpit and windows. From underneath, there emitted several jets of vapour or 'steam' and the crew at first appeared perfectly human, wearing silver jump suits with polo necks and a zip from the waist up to the neck on the right-hand side.

The craft's interior was illuminated with a dull light and from some kind of hatch, the eldest member of the trio inside now stepped out and walked over to the increasingly terrified Mrs Bowles and her passenger.

The 'Ufonaut' was quite tall, about six foot two inches, Joyce estimated. He appeared to be about 45-years-old by our standard, and he wore long fair hair down to the shoulder, somewhere between silver and auburn in colouring continuing into sideburns which ended in a Van Dyke beard.

He reached the car and rested his left arm on the roof while looking in at the occupants. Joyce could see he had pale, clear white skin, but his eyes frightened her. They were pink, like an albino rabbit, with practically no iris showing. Ted Pratt, however, thought he looked a very ordinary chap, calm and non-aggressive.

As he approached the Mini, Mrs Bowles had noticed a high-pitched, whistling sound that seemed associated with the figure. However, despite his apparent attempt to calm the couple, Mrs Bowles, stressed by the alarming circumstances of this man's arrival, became quite hysterical and wrapped herself around Mr Pratt, pleading with him not to open the car door and talk to the stranger, which was his first inclination.

At this point, the 'visitor' now looked at the dashboard of the Clubman with a penetrating gaze and, without any human action, the engine suddenly started and ran for a couple of minutes, even though the ignition key was turned off. At the same time, the headlamps, which had been left on, inexplicably shone an estimated four times brighter than normal.

Throughout the encounter, Ted Pratt remained strangely in control. He recalled, "The man looked at me and I think transmitted some power which calmed me."

Mrs Bowles was also aware of some power from the stranger apart from the whistle, since after looking into his eyes, she experienced spots of light in front of her as if she had been looking at a lamp filament. She also noticed the stranger seemed to have a thicker cornea than in a normal eye.

In the confusion, Mrs Bowles still hiding her head and seeking the protection of Ted, they were vaguely aware that the figure had moved to the rear of the car. Ted looked around his left shoulder expecting the Ufonaut to appear on his side. But he failed to do so, and the craft somehow disappeared along with its occupants. Ted and Joyce could no longer see the UFO in the darkness that surrounded them, stabbed only by the now normal illumination from the headlamps.

Turning down Ted's offer to drive her home, as this would mean opening the car doors to change places, Joyce started the engine, which fired normally, and tried to move off, but the 'invisible barrier' still seemed to be in operation and the car refused to budge. She waited a couple of minutes and tried again; this time all was normal and they left the scene, arriving at their destination at 9:02 p.m. The encounter had lasted no more than five or six minutes, but it had seemed like hours to the frightened travellers.

Their tyre impressions were visible in the mud the next day and over the next week, the encounter seems to have been corroborated by reports from other motorists who also saw the UFO.

Charles Privitt of Southampton writes:

> "Just a short time ago, some people reported a UFO on the Winchester bypass. On the same night, I was travelling home from my girlfriend's house. I saw what I would swear on any oath to be a UFO. It was 11 p.m. and I was about three miles from the bypass, on a hill. I've seen reflections from other car lights on mist or fog, or even on the clouds. Eastleigh has an airport, so I know a plane with its flashing red and green lights and also its white headlights. What I saw was none of these. I'm not a drinker either.
>
> "Coming across from the bypass area was an orange-red light at about 100-feet, not flashing but glowing like a main street light, hard to focus on. It was round, sort of loaf shaped, so silent, because I slowed

down in my car and coasted to see if I could hear any noise. It came towards me, went over my car and disappeared in the Petersfield direction over the wooded area."

Mr S. W. Freemantle of Southampton also tells us:

"Back in January, I went and investigated the site of the reported landing of a space craft at Chilcomb, at the end of the Winchester bypass. I spent about two hours there on the Wednesday morning and after a while, found a few faint footprints leading from the field where the craft landed, to the point where the car went up on the grass. They were about our size with plain soles, but each one was about six-inches or so longer in the stride than our average stride.

"If they were 'his' then he must have been quite tall with a long stride. I was asked not to go into the field where the craft was reported landed, as it had been ploughed. But it was about 75-yards from the edge, and there seemed to be a depression in this area about 20-feet across. But as we had had a lot of rain, it was very difficult to tell. Still, I enjoyed my two hours of searching around."

Whether the footprints or the apparent 'depression' in the adjoining field are relevant we cannot tell as the 'craft' could have touched down prior to, or after the event just off the road, on the other side of the hedgerow.

According to Mrs Bowles, the Mini now performs better than it did before the strange encounter and the watch she was wearing that night now gains unaccountably. She broke out in a blotchy rash on her right shoulder, arm and neck the following day and also could not eat for three days. She remained somewhat shaken over the incident and could not decide whether the rash was a result of her 'meeting' or nerves. However, she had not suffered from the trouble before and generally felt better in health and vitality after the incident.

After the terrifying events of 14th November, Joyce was quite content to forget the unwelcome attentions of her strange visitors, but fate was not to have it so. The evening of 30th December 1976, from 6:45 p.m. on, was to yield the next scene of the now widely-publicised 'Winchester Mystery'.

Mrs Bowles and Ted Pratt had gone out in the Mini to get some petrol and were travelling between her home and Chilcomb, when they again saw an orange light in the sky. They turned a corner and without reason, the car started to rock backwards and forwards and yaw from side-to-side. This was accompanied by a high-pitched whistle, similar to the noise Joyce had heard on the first occasion.

There then seems to be a segment of time missing and a loss of memory by both witnesses, because the next they can remember is being inside a dome-shaped chamber about 14-feet-high.

The Mini Clubman was with them in the chamber and they were standing beside it. Also with them were three of the 'aliens', including the same '45-year-old' man who had approached Ted and Joyce on the first occasion. All the UFO's crew were dressed alike in silver boiler suits that seemed to be slightly inflated, but they wore no helmets and Joyce and Ted had no difficulty breathing, indicating a compatibility of atmospheres.

The occupants also wore gloves that fitted tightly around their wrists. The trousers were also tight-fitting and were tucked into ankle boots. Their entire outfits glowed with a soft phosphorescence.

All had the same fair, sandy-haired colouring. The eldest man, who appeared in charge, also had a belt containing a circular, iridescent, faceted lens which he often touched as if adjusting it.

The younger 'aliens' were clean-shaven, unlike their 'captain' who retained the small beard he had worn on the occasion of the first meeting.

They spoke among themselves in a slightly oriental-sounding language that Ted and Joyce did not understand. The only word they remember was something like 'Mi-Lee-Ga'. The senior member then addressed them in accented, broken English.

Mr Pratt was requested to take seven paces forward towards a rotating central column, around which were displayed symbols similar to those used in astrology. The column itself was coloured red and black and as Ted approached it, he noticed the air felt warmer.

To one side of this machine sat one of the crew, operating a control desk with numerous multi-coloured, flashing lights predominantly blue in appearance. On the wall of the chamber were curious charts of circles and lines.

The 'captain' referred to these and commented, "This is our field," although in what context was not clear.

Upon returning from the column, Ted found the temperature to be cool again and the leader reassured him, stating, "We are not hostile towards you, you must tell the world," to which Joyce replied something to the effect that "Hitler said that," and she was rebuked with, "You have a very strong tongue," from the captain.

Ted also asked why they had picked Joyce and it was indicated that the Mini had been marked in some way. The aliens also made it clear that they would return on another occasion, but did not say when.

During this conversation, Joyce was able to observe their supposedly extra-terrestrial host at close quarters. His fair, almost transparent, skin was flawless and his nose thin and long, but the eyes were the only features that might identify him as not from Earth. The pupil, under normal light conditions, almost disappeared to nothing, whereas it had been over-naturally large in the darkness of the initial encounter. This suggested, together with his skin complexion, an origin from a planet or environment of lower light levels than we usually enjoy here. The coolness inside the 'craft' might also lend weight to this theory, as well as the predominately nocturnal pattern of the worldwide UFO activity.

Joyce remembers that the Ufonaut conveyed more information to Mr Pratt but most of it he didn't understand. The next thing she can recall is a strange, powerful beam of white light shining through the Mini from the rear and out from the windscreen. She then remembered suddenly waking up inside the car, parked beside a river somewhere outside Winchester, but on a different side of the town to where they had last been driving.

They could see car headlamps in the distance and drove towards them, eventually finding their way home in the darkness. They arrived home at 8:15 p.m. having lost over an hour of their lives for which they could not fully account.

The Ufonauts did indeed return, this time when Mrs Bowles was driving with another family friend, Ann Stickland of Southampton on 10th March 1977. However, before this, another UFO sighting had been observed by Miss G. Britain, and two friends at Portchester, just west of Portsmouth, on 7th January.

Miss Britain, who lives on a caravan site near Portchester Crematorium, described the UFO as a "...pink ball with a white light in the middle". It landed in a field near her then there was a puff of smoke and she saw a low-flying object zoom away over the horizon. She found the incident alarming enough to report it to the police. The only conventional explanation put forward was that the sighting may have been a student hoax produced by a large pink plastic bag filled with hot air generated by a candle inside. However, a conclusive identification could not be made as little notice was taken of the report and no investigation made at the time.

But returning to the not-so-easy-to-explain encounter of Joyce Bowles and Ann Stickland. The Mini Clubman that was now, apparently, singled out for special attention by the 'aliens', seemed to be the key factor allowing the location of the 'contactees' to be monitored.

The two women reported that the car was intercepted by another of the cigar-shaped UFOs, but this time in daylight, at 10.15 a.m. Ann was in Hampshire with Joyce, who was driving them northwards to visit friends on Monday 7th March, when suddenly the car slowed down and came to a halt.

Both women got out of the car to see if they could find the trouble, when they became aware of a large light, glaring like the sun, across the road in front of them. It appeared to be coming from a large oval object on the ground nearby that appeared to be the same kind of craft.

A man stepped out from the oval craft and walked towards Mrs Bowles. He was about six-feet-tall, again with long, sandy hair, dressed in an all-in-one, shiny suit. He had what looked like a belt around his waist, with a sparkling light resembling a diamond in the centre. He came up to Joyce, took both her hands in his and began to talk to her in what sounded like broken English. At this point, he looked at Ann for a moment and she found she could not move. He continued to talk to Mrs Bowles after which he turned and walked back towards the craft.

Halfway back, he turned and raised his arm and pointed to them. Ann was then able to move normally. As they got back into the car, the craft moved sideways across the road and suddenly disappeared. The car started with no trouble and they turned around and headed for home.

Throughout the meeting, both witnesses had been aware of a high-pitched humming that rose to a scream when the craft took off.

Mrs Bowles stated that the 'spaceman's' hands, apparently not gloved on this occasion, "…were warm, like a human being's". However, the following day, both her hands swelled up and she also complained of a bad chest.

She recognised the Ufonaut as the same man who had approached her on previous occasions, but he had grown his hair longer and now it flowed down over his shoulders.

The witnesses were mainly worried that he would return and 'take them off' permanently. This fear was prompted by the message given to Joyce on the third contact. After some difficulty in making her understand, apparently the alien alarmingly implied that, "You are one of us," leaving her confused and in something of a state of shock.

I, myself, would think the remark was intended more in the general sense, rather than to Joyce Bowles personally, and may indicate more about the origins of mankind than we at present understand or admit.

Apparently, a fourth and as far as I am aware, final contact, took place in May 1977, when Mrs Bowles was again accompanied by Ted Pratt. This time two of the same red-haired Ufonauts conveyed 'messages' regarding their concern about the nuclear situation here on Earth.

By this time, the witnesses were experiencing some harassment from the press and UFO enthusiasts and were becoming more reluctant to speak about their experiences. However, there is one very important factor peripheral to these four encounters—the continued gamut of psychic phenomena taking place in Mrs Bowles' presence. This ranged from mild to heavy poltergeist activity, an apparent capacity for psychic healing, levitation of small objects and the occasional materialisation of ghostly forms, some of which were visible to other people. These all happened on an irregular basis, and may suggest that Joyce Bowles was a latent source of powerful psychic energy.

It may well be that the origin of the events of the 'Winchester Mystery', lie more in the breaking through of some supernatural or alternate dimension. The observations in Hampshire do have a place in some kind of reality, even if it only overlaps ours for short transient periods of time, for other people were also seeing inexplicable things that came out of the sky. For instance, Irene Armstrong of Aldershot, who reports:

> "I wonder if you can inform me as to whether I had optical illusion or if in reality I did see a UFO. Yesterday morning, 28th March, around 9 a.m., I went into the kitchen and casually glanced up at the top window pane. Through it, I saw a strange object. I looked away and then thought, 'Ah! What's that?' I then looked back again, but nothing was to be seen. I forgot about it, thinking I'd probably had an optical illusion.
>
> "During the evening, I suddenly thought about this experience and mentioned it to my son. He informed me that UFOs were sometimes seen like this, but I replied as to how could I possibly see in so much detail in the course of a split second? The morning of the sighting was fine, and a very large white cloud was in the sky. The object was against the cloud and crescent-shaped at the front. I saw a hollow indentation in the centre, it was like a half-cigar in shape."

Shortly afterwards in April 1977, the Minister of Defence took this borderland of reality seriously enough to order an investigation into a sighting by Trinity House pilot's assistant Rod Riddell and his wife Jenny, from their home at Ryde, Isle of Wight.

They reported, 'a rectangular hovercraft without windows' that first appeared as a 'bright light', which then approached their house and hung, suspended, at about an altitude of 300-feet. The sighting occurred just after midnight and the craft, after remaining stationary for a few moments, then picked up speed and flashed out of sight.

The Ministry of Defence would probably have a little difficulty in identifying a hovercraft, that was capable of flying at speed, at a height of 300-feet!

Chapter 6: Behind The Welsh Triangle

Perhaps the real story behind 'The Welsh Triangle' is expressed by D. W. Trow of Merthyr Tydfil when he said, "I've seen strange sightings but have said nothing, people only laugh."

There is very little to laugh about in the curious and alarming events that have been transpiring in South Wales over the past years.

The detailed story is covered in my books '*The Welsh Triangle*,' and '*The Welsh Triangle Revisited*', but to put the occurrences in some kind of historical perspective, this report from George Hortop, of Barry, would indicate that the coast along the Bristol Channel has been the scene of UFO activity for some years. He writes in considerable detail:

> 'The flying saucer incident we witnessed occurred on 6th August 1954 in the early evening. Time noted down as 17.45 hours. Both of us were sitting on the pebble beach at The Knap, Barry, when our attention was taken by a stationary object over the Bristol

Channel in a south west direction well out past Rhoose Point. This object was a brilliant silver colour and conveyed the impression of a strong light reflecting on a chromium or silver body.

"The thing that struck us, was that although there was a slight westerly wind the object, disc-shaped, was not moving. The weather was perfect for any August evening, the sky was exceptionally blue and clear of cloud apart from one or two small patches of fractocumulus cloud, so more or less broad daylight as you can imagine. Also take note that this sighting was witnessed, as we both found out later on in the week through the national press, by a considerable number of keen and experienced observers at RAF St Athan and Rhoose Airport.

"Members of the RAF Gliding School were completing a series of flying operations from St Athan airfield at the time. The commanding officer, several instructors and a number of air cadets were present; all of whom bore witness to the entity that appeared over the Bristol Channel that August evening in 1954. A flying officer, it was stated, took off in a glider with a pupil to investigate the object from a closer angle and I quote his words: "*The form I observed was that of a large double-convex lens viewed in vertical profile. It was not possible to estimate its true size or distance at which it was stationed, but on the southern and eastern legs of the first circuit of which I flew, the object was perfectly clear against a blue sky and very sharply defined and a bright silver colour."*

"Another thing that impressed the officer flying near the object, as he stated, was the immobility of the thing. It remained quite stationary and was seemingly unaffected by wind or air currents. This, of course, was also the talking point between my fiance while I was watching it from the pebble beach.

"The officer landed after one circuit and took off again with the same cadet for a second circuit similar to the first. During this flight towards the object they found it was in the same position but had altered its shape to that of a silvery dumbbell. There was no apparent approach or recession or lateral movement of the form over the critical six to seven minutes of observation from the glider. This discounted the idea that it could be light from a conventional aircraft.

"The immobility of the object equally discouraged the idea that it was a free meteorological balloon. From the beach, we could not see it changing shape but could pick out the glider near it. On this last circuit by the glider, the object suddenly vanished. On the beach we had been watching this object for an estimated two hours when we noticed it disappear. This aerial phenomenon really baffled us both. For a daylight sighting, this was unique, as it is for an aircraft to get such a good close up of such a phenomenon."

It was not until the mid-1970s that reports really started flowing in from Wales on a regular basis. Typical was this letter from C. B. Griffiths of Rhymney, Gwent:

"Late in 1975 while watching a TV film in a darkened room, my wife spotted something in the sky through the window. A lovely red glow filled the room and then I saw a beautiful red circle of light with a blue surround. Outside it was clear cut like the setting sun. No sound, no sparks. Then it just seemed to switch off and disappear."

Compare this sighting from young Anthony Roderick of Cwmtame:

"I saw a UFO in 1976. I had been in a disco and I was very tired and hot so I went outside for fresh air. After I had been out there for a long time I was joined by my pals. I looked up at the stars and at the moon. It was a nice clear night. Then about 200-feet up we saw a blue object. It went on and off and it was like two soup plates stuck together. It hovered above us and then moved off quickly and then disappeared. It had a black hole under the bottom.

"We shouted up, all of us laughing and shouting, 'UFO!' When it had gone, I felt scared. My friend went home and we met in school next day. He said that his brother saw a UFO too, zooming, stop, then go away. We took it to be the same UFO we saw."

On 12th December 1976, things were warming up in Wales, commencing with this precise report from Tony Heare of Pontypool:

"I saw a blue/white light at the front of an object with a red/orange light flashing directly above and three or four blue/white lights behind the first. It gave the impression of being vaguely similar to the size of a single decker bus. No noise was audible at all. A car moved off nearby, but soon all was quiet again. The object was seen from the car park of Llandegweth reservoir, facing towards Newport.

"The object travelled on a seemingly straight line. It just reached a mountain to our right, seeming to hover, then turned on its axis and travelled back towards our left. We hardly needed to look up to see the object. It appeared to be over somewhere between Cwmbran and Newport a distance from us of about two miles. The weather was cloudy, but the object was definitely below cloud cover. There was no haze or fog present. The speed of the object was very slow indeed, comparable to that of a helicopter or a small plane, but no noise was audible. I have not notified the police or any local authority about sighting."

By the early days of February 1977, indications were obvious that a 'UFO flap' was about to break out. One object was seen by at least a dozen independent observers, including Mr and Mrs G. D. Withey of Blackwood, Gwent, who wrote:

"I would like to inform you of the sightings of two unidentified flying objects. The first was sighted by my wife and I from our kitchen window on the morning of Tuesday, 1st February 1977, at approximately 7:45 a.m. Our house is situated in a high position overlooking the town of Blackwood and surrounding area, with our kitchen facing east. The sky was clear, with no clouds and the object was sighted before the sun had risen over the horizon. The object was cigar-shaped and orange in colour and appeared to be moving slowly in a north-easterly direction over the Mynyddislwyn Mountains, to the east of our house. It stayed in view for approximately five minutes before disappearing over the horizon, and during that time, something on the edge was shining or reflecting the sun.

"The second object was sighted as we were travelling from Blackwood in our car, ten minutes later. It was the same shape as the first object and moving approximately the same speed and in the same direction. Its colour was white but changed to orange as it went over the horizon. The reason for the delay in writing since the sightings is because we didn't know who to get in touch with about them."

Two days later Mrs Jessie Morris of Swansea had her own UFO experience:

"On 3rd February 1977, I had a phone call from a relative at 10:15 a.m., telling me about a strange bright object below the clouds, a couple of hundred feet up. The glow was blinding and vanished after seven minutes. His wife also saw it, but a strange thing happened while the UFO was visible. His legs and feet became numb, and afterwards he could not walk for three hours. It was above Ystradgynlais, Powys, just over the Dyfed border, and there are reservoirs not far away, also a high tension electrical installation."

The next day the first of the classic 'Welsh Triangle' sightings was made by the Broadhaven schoolchildren. From the 14 drawings sketched independently by the youngsters after their experience, a number of reasonable common denominators seemed evident.

The craft was gently dome-shaped with a cupola on its upper surface. Underneath, it seems likely that the surface was also curved, hence the craft had been very much like two china saucers put together, but with the bulk of the craft being on the upper side. Nearly everyone agreed that at the top central point there was a red, flashing light. Most agreed that somewhere near the centre a dark opening or hatch had appeared and from this at least one occupant had emerged. It also seemed that the top cupola may have had some kind of apertures, or even port-holes on it, although no one could agree on how many there were.

As to the occupant of the craft, there seemed only general agreement that he had been wearing a kind of silvery suit, but he was at least of relatively normal human appearance. No facial or other bodily details had been noted, due to the distance of the object. His helmet and I suspected the UFO's appearance had produced some pandemonium to say the least.

Later, another landing was reported by Mrs Josephine Hewison at her farm outside Little Haven, at the heart of the 'Triangle'.

The object stayed only a few minutes and while Josephine was hurriedly dressing to take a closer look at her uninvited guests, it departed in a couple of seconds.

Despite searching, she could find no trace of it having been in the paddock. She wasn't surprised about this because slurry and mud from heavy rain the previous night would quickly have obscured any marks, although the morning had brought blue sky and bright sunshine.

Another series of mysterious events in the 'Welsh

Triangle' also happened just outside Little Haven.

A prominent and well-respected hotelier had a startling series of encounters involving craft landing on her property and physical damage to her buildings. This also occurred close to a Royal Observer Corps nuclear fall-out shelter. So anxious and concerned were the witnesses that they wrote to their Member of Parliament.

A revealing series of communications and incidents followed, resulting in a personal visit by a very high-ranking RAF officer. He came alone, except for his driver who waited outside, and was so intensely interested in the account that he spent several hours meticulously documenting the details on to hand-written forms. When pressed for answers by the witnesses he gave his own opinion of the reality of the phenomena, but asked them to keep the whole affair secret.

However, follow-up enquiries by the hotelier to her MP and to the Under Secretary of State for Defence told a different story. It was evident some of the information was deemed so delicate that not even Parliament was being told the whole truth.

However, the principle mysteries of the 'Triangle' occurred at Ripperston Farm, West Wales. This particular locale was so rich in events that the resident herdsman and his family had difficulty in recalling the precise dates when the numerous incidents had occurred.

Some very strange things had been happening down on the farm. At least three cows had completely disappeared. Not so very uncommon, you might think in this day of modern rustlers, but this particular farm is reached by a private track and the only access is right by the farm cottage. It is bordered on its western perimeter by cliffs that are doubly-fenced to prevent cows accidentally tumbling off the edge into the sea. Furthermore, the farm's fields are individually-fenced and the cows in question were nowhere near the sea when they vanished.

The whole herd, or parts of it at various times, had also completely 'de-materialised'. I was present at the farmhouse, when one particular incident took place, although not actually an eyewitness to the event. Various members of the farm staff had secured the cows in the large, covered shed but just a few moments later they found they had mysteriously appeared in an outdoor paddock. Given the distance between the two locations, it would have been impossible for them to muster in the field in the time that had elapsed, even if the cowshed hadn't been locked!

In another startling example, the herdsman left 158 cows in this cowshed and walked to his cottage where he found the telephone ringing. On lifting the receiver, he was informed by a neighbour that his cows were eating crops half-a-mile away. With mild incredulity he told him that this was quite impossible, but went to check the cowshed anyway, only to find it completely empty except for a thin blue mist.

For the animals to have left the enclosure, they

would have had to pass him on his way to the farm cottage, there being no other way out. But for them to have travelled over several hedgerows to the adjoining farm could easily have taken half-an-hour. Yet all of this had transpired in under a minute. Small wonder that people in the area were reluctant to relate their more intimate experiences.

Indeed, the down-to-earth sanity and rural common sense that I found among these people, and that's somewhat lacking in our cities today, was most impressive. It was obvious that they literally did not believe the evidence of their own eyes. Often an air of reverence, even awe, seemed to enter the conversations when relating their experiences. But relate them they did and I shall always be indebted to the trust and sincerity shown towards me by these people. They ranged from the very old to the very young. The innocent wonder on the children's faces is something I shall never forget.

They recounted seeing silvered disc-shaped craft silently, stealthily descend from the skies, gleaming in the sunlight, completely untroubled by our defence systems. From these craft emerged tall space-suited individuals who walked about, approaching some of the children who naturally hid or ran away.

The problem often seemed not to discover who had seen a UFO, but rather to actually come across somebody who had not.

At Haverfordwest police station, always a bastion of common sense and reliability, I quizzed the local police for their reaction. Of the men in the office three had actually seen UFOs themselves. Everybody accepted the reality of the phenomena; indeed, the question of its unreality seemed laughable. However, I was somewhat alarmed when I enquired as to the procedure for dealing with these matters. Calmly, a sergeant looked at me with an inscrutable expression and said, "There is no procedure, Sir." Nothing further seemed necessary to be said. The authorities seemed faced with a situation for which no provision had ever been made, and because no provision had ever been made no provision could be made. Officially it did not exist!

One final comment was made by a detective inspector, "After what I've seen round here nothing would surprise me," he said.

When I was learning to fly many years ago, visibility was one of the basic concerns of all pilots. It was the one thing you depended on. Instruments or no, you wanted to see where you were going. So enquiries at Haverfordwest aerodrome, a small civilian establishment, surprised me when a local pilot volunteered the information, "We have the worst bloody weather in the British Isles.

"I haven't been able to get off the ground for five days this week," he complained bitterly. This bore out my own observations, after having been in the area several months. The Atlantic weather bombards this coastal Pembroke peninsula almost continuously; it never seems to stop raining. When it did, the warming effect of the sea brought in coastal fog.

So the revelation in a local paper that the RAF operated a pilot training school on the coast seemed strange. Surely they would be more suited to the happy hunting ground of the Central Flying School of East Anglia, where the sun shines more days than not. What were they doing on this windy, wet, foggy, western outpost?

The RAF had only been there a short time. In fact, the station had been closed down for a short period. It used to belong to the Royal Navy.

Now that made sense. The Navy fly at sea, they fly in poor conditions and therefore it was logical that they should gain experience on a coastal station, simulating conditions to which they were likely to be exposed.

More contradictions arose, but somebody reassured me, 'It was a political decision.'

Apparently, the married quarters were going to be sold to the council and local people had looked forward to the sudden availability of new homes. Everything went according to plan on the Navy's departure, then suddenly it was all reversed. Now the houses were full of military personnel yet again, this time Americans!

I had noticed the odd couple of Americans floating about Haverfordwest. They always stick out like a sore thumb in broad check jackets, US shoes and haircuts. I could almost predict which state they came from. Apparently the Americans operated some sort of secret oceanographic research station on the coast which employed a good number of geologists. Now that sounded interesting...

The local library was the obvious source of public information. I spent many an hour combing its archives and the results were fascinating.

The area had scattered disused mines. My analysis of the UFOs' activities indicated an interest in underground installations. This, together with the comments of the Coombs family, one of the most involved and closely-encountered of the witnesses, the problem was clarified a little further.

"One day I saw the sea shake," Mrs Combs had stated. "Not waves you understand, but actual vibrations." As she lives right on the edge of the Atlantic coast overlooking a notably calm stretch of sheltered ocean, I figured that she knew what she was talking about.

Who was mining in St. Brides Bay? Celtic Oil? Unlikely. That was a red herring, obviously. Someone was prospecting for bigger fish!

One thing you had to get used to while on the Pembrokeshire coast was the 'boom'. Not so much of a boom as a rumble. Concorde, you might be told knowledgeably by an, 'informed' local. As your windows shook and your glasses jangled and the floorboards vibrated violently under your feet, you could be reassured 'officially' that this was Concorde.

I am something of a patron of air shows and aircraft in general. I think I know a sonic boom when I hear one. My first reaction to the Welsh boom was to run for the door.

An earth tremor? I recalled a similar happening while climbing a volcano in Italy, a disquieting experience as the world seems to vibrate around you. It had lasted several seconds.

Slightly shaken, I was to become so used to the 'boom' that I would hardly bother to look out of the window, as it became an almost daily occurrence. The enigma was not a new one. My files already contained an extensive batch of clippings on a mysterious boom that had been heard on both sides of the Bristol Channel.

Indeed, the whole thing seems to have started off by a story based on the village of North Petherton, where people had complained of similar vibrations. Extensive investigation by the University of Bristol had revealed little and the findings were contradictory. The boom had occurred on nights when neither the British nor French Concorde was flying and in early research it was declared that the harmonic pattern of the vibration was in no way similar to that produced by a high-flying aircraft. Later proclamations by the authorities declared complete certainty that the culprit was Concorde.

But one felt that either the problem was being filed away under a familiar heading or lost in a bland statement. I had noticed that as public interest had increased in the 'boom' its occurrence had been synchronised with Concorde flights. At the time I made nothing of this. Perhaps I should have done.

There appeared to be two kinds of booms:

supersonic boom and undercover activity. As long as the undercover one synchronised with the acceptable and correctly-timed explainable boom, nobody was going to worry about anything.

Returning to the trail of UFOs, it isn't impossible that accidents in time can occur. That people, things and particles do irrationally disappear and possibly reappear at some later point, without any effective ageing. But it also seems likely to me that some of these events are arranged, in fact openly engineered, by various intelligences. We can only speculate on their motives and cultural beliefs.

In a very advanced civilisation, the element of play and pure curiosity may be of more importance than an emphasis towards working to live. While in our 20th (now 21st) Century society, we are intelligent beings but preoccupied with earning a living, a highly evolved society is likely to be freed from solving practical daily living concerns. Comparatively, understanding their mentality and outlook may be as challenging for us as understanding the structure of intelligent, but utterly different, dolphin society.

In the case of the 'Welsh Triangle', we have a classic example of every type of 'contact', whether it is with an intelligence from outer space or from some parallel universe. Additionally, the area itself, historically and traditionally, has a certain undefined peculiarity.

I'm not going to pretend that the 'Welsh Triangle' is a 'one-off' unique area of the world. I think it is a demonstration of something that occurs in many places, for example the Bermuda Triangle or the China Sea. Here in England, we've seen that there are areas that also attract exceptional events of peculiar strangeness, including Warminster in Wiltshire and also parts of East Anglia. None of these areas have definite boundaries, but I think that conditions within them seem to attract more esoteric events.

Neither am I suggesting that any of the events I am relating in this book are the result of supernatural spectres or imagined hauntings. These events were factual and the effects that they had were solid. The extra-terrestrials—for I am convinced that the majority of the activity belongs strictly in their camp—are solid flesh and blood. They do, however, have highly-developed technological capabilities and an understanding of the workings of energy and matter. This can make many of their actions appear more magical and illusionary than real.

Humans have developed the processes of fission and the conversion of matter into energy. The events in West Wales demonstrate that the intelligence that controls the UFOs has mastered the counter-effect, the production of matter out of energy. The total control of energy as a structure within itself, and the manipulation of those subtle influences that can affect the human mind and even matter directly without mechanical application.

The well-known spoon-benders such as Uri Geller and Jean-Pierre Girard have demonstrated that the human mind can directly affect metals, instruments and even computers. Along with countless other psychics such as Matthew Manning and the amazing experiments done in Russia into telekinesis, I think it is clearly demonstrated that we are now on the threshold of a major breakthrough in mental control of matter. It is largely a random process at the moment, but the Russians are working very hard to turn it to some practical use, almost certainly for military objectives.

However, if the motives are not all that desirable, the spin-off in terms of our cultural understanding may be startling. How much of this research is based on studies of events occurring throughout history is open to speculation. But to dismiss their reality out of hand, as is done by some entrenched academic thinkers, is as irrational as the papal attitude in the Middle Ages, which declared that to think the world was a sphere and no longer the centre of the universe was heresy.

Back in Wales, in the backyard of Ripperston Farm, herdsman Billy Coombs witnessed an event that was beyond his understanding. It was an event that instantly trans-located 158 cows nearly a mile without any physical assistance and appeared to transcend the function of time. The 'Welsh Triangle' had thrown up an event that had occurred elsewhere in the world, but in this particular instance I believe the event was engineered; it was an experiment involving and performed by UFO intelligences.

We use animals extensively in experiments ourselves, prior to human application in our medicine and science. In the particular event at Ripperston Farm, none of the animals suffered any harmful physical effects although their milk yield did drop dramatically. It would seem to me that some intelligence was proving a point to itself, not as a demonstration, for little publicity emerged from it. But the experiment was a simple one to see if, in certain circumstances upon which we can only speculate, it would be possible to instantly move a large quantity of living organic creatures from one location to another. The mechanism by which one could undertake this task is a matter for hypothesis.

However, one must remember that the space between atoms is as great as the space between stars. Our understanding of matter as a solid reality has now advanced to the idea that atoms are really only projections of energy waveforms, that all is really fluid, as fluid as the water that comes out of the tap and almost as intangible as the air we breathe or the light from the stars. It may be possible that some advanced technology has found a method of by-passing physical matter in its obvious form, and that in fact the cows never really lost their physical structure between one place and the other but arrived by some re-arrangement of time and space?

When I was engaged in a little fundamental particle research at Birmingham University in conjunction with CERN, I found that sub-atomic particles appeared and disappeared. We had a host of explanations for it in terms of various interactions. But I often wondered if our theories were really chasing the cat by the tail, trying to find logical explanations for events that we really did not fully understand. The investigators of sub-atomic physics seem to be endeavouring to find ever-more complex explanations in order to explain all the numerous, and quite inexplicable, events that occur in laboratories every day. We are now asked to consider that some sub-atomic particles have consciousness, that some know what to do all by themselves.

In our short lives lasting but a mere 80 or so years, we are really looking at the universe as a single snapshot, one frame of a film that continues forever. Our ability to perceive the movement is as difficult as trying to watch a plant grow, but grow and move intelligently it does.

As our scientific knowledge has advanced over the past 50 years, scientists are gradually understanding the extreme subtleties controlling the vastness of space. The planets and stars *must* be connected and *must* interact—not only via gravitational and energy waves, but possibly by something even faster; an 'instant knowing' that permits the keeping of order.

I am proposing that beyond our present levels of communications and interaction, there is an alien intelligence whose vast knowledge of universal physics allows them interstellar travel to many destinations, including our own blue planet. Indeed, many of these intelligences seem to be here quite often or even on a permanent basis.

Chapter 7: Mystery Of The Moors

Already rich in supernatural phenomena, the West Country moors have proved a rich source of some of the most intriguing close encounters with strange other-worldly craft. From the tip of Cornwall to the heart of Somerset, everyday folk have come forward with tales of experiences with men and machines not of human ken.

Typical of the mysteries is this account from the Somerset-based investigator and researcher into the unknown, my old colleague, Ed Harris:

> "The phenomenon had been going on for five days when we investigated the sighting. It always happened around seven or eight in the evening. A light would appear from the west, traverse the sky at a 'steady' pace, and come to rest over the church. After staying still for up to five minutes, the light would pass on and disappear into the distance, still going in a straight line.
>
> "The sixth night of the occurrence, my companions and I attended and at a little after 7:10 p.m. we saw the already

mentioned light appear from over some trees. It was of a dull, yellowish hue, and it wasn't until I focused on it with my binoculars that I realised that it appeared to be pulsating slightly. Its outer edges were clearly defined against the night sky. In fact, the moonlight seemed to reflect off it, rather in the way that it would off metal.

"I watched, fascinated, as the light came to rest, as it always did, above the church, the whole light changing colour to a deep orange and starting to rotate, staying stationary in the sky. Then a dark patch appeared on the light and seemed to extend down towards the ground, stopping no more than six-feet above the tower of the church! Thoroughly perplexed as to what it was, I moved towards the church, taking my eyes off it for a moment to undo a catch on the gate. When I looked back the light had assumed its former yellowish colour and had re-started on its journey across the sky. I was completely baffled and after asking one or two of those present what they'd seen; I wasn't enlightened any.

"The vicar kindly let me up the church tower the next day, but I found nothing there, save that some of the wind-blown leaves were blackened as if they'd been burned, and in fact, disintegrated to dust upon me touching them!"

Other mystery lights were seen over St Austell,

Cornwall, by Mr C. Matthews, who writes:

> "I have seen several strange lights in the sky here in Cornwall. Some of the reports I have read confirm or closely resemble my own sightings, especially the faint hissing sound made by these objects.
>
> "On one occasion while I was out for a walk one evening, I followed a light in the sky that was travelling in a northerly direction. At first I thought it might be a plane but then it stopped dead as though hovering. It then started off in westerly direction towards me. The sky was absolutely clear, no cloud, a brilliant starry night, so I stood still and waited, listening for engines. It passed almost over me at an estimated height of two-and-a-half thousand feet. By now there were a pair of lights one behind the other, no bigger than the stars in the background. If they belonged to the same object, which I assumed they did as they were travelling at identical speed, it would have been colossal in length, I would say about 60-feet long. All I could hear was a faint hiss, but the strangest part was there was no shape to the object, as though it was invisible except for the lights.
>
> "I could see the stars between the lights and all around them, which would have been impossible if it had been a plane. This was reported by someone else and a report was

also printed in The Guardian a couple of days afterwards. It was passed off as American tanker refuelling flights, which to me was ridiculous. A single jet would make ten times more noise than this object. Its speed was not fast, almost coasting along. This is only one of the strange sightings I have witnessed."

One of the most famous West Country sightings was the 'Flying Cross' sighted by motor patrol police constables, Clifford Waycott and Roger Willey from Okehampton, in the early hours of an October morning in 1967.

On observing the object at 4 a.m., the policemen checked it was not a reflection by stopping and watching the amazingly brilliant machine from outside their car. When it moved off, they gave chase and followed it for 14 miles at speeds of up to 70 mph down the darkened, lonely Dartmoor roads. They eventually lost it as it flashed away at only treetop height.

However, it showed up further west over Truro, Cornwall, where it was seen by the Reverend Ian Haile, and later at Lancing, where P.C. Michael Sands saw it at 5:20 a.m. By 6 a.m. it was over London and was reported by Elizabeth Cole of Maidenhead:

> "It was hanging over London. I had been waiting till six o'clock to get up and make some tea as my husband was away and I had not slept well. Instead of going straight

> out of the door I did a very strange thing. I went to the window and pulled back the curtains. There it was! Just like a huge brilliant star. I went out on the balcony and looked at it through binoculars and it was a perfect circle. It was darker in the centre and had pinpoints of light evenly all around. As I watched, the top third disappeared. The milkman came and as I was in my dressing gown I came indoors. It could have been telepathy which made me pull the curtains back. I've never done it before or since, as I am not one bit interested in the weather."

Earlier in 1967, another huge UFO had been reported by coastguards at Brixham, Devon; on the morning of 28th April. It is estimated that the cone shaped UFO held its position for nearly an hour against a strong breeze. During this time, hundreds of people along the Torbay coast caught sight of it and an RAF jet was seen to intercept it, but it climbed away through cloud and disappeared around 20,000 feet.

A senior RAF controller at Plymouth said of the jet scramble:

> "We reported all the details. I cannot tell you where the aircraft came from and you will have a job to get anyone to admit that one was sent up, I understand the UFO was also tracked by radar."

A Ministry of Defence spokesman volunteered of

the midday sighting:

> "We can only suggest that the object may have been a reflection of car headlights or some sort of meteorological phenomenon."

But coastguard Brian Jenkins was unconvinced by the 'off the shelf' explanation. He said of the UFO at the time:

> "I was able to make a detailed drawing of it which I showed to an air vice-marshal who called at the station a few days later. His only comment was 'most interesting'"

Two 'orange discs' were also seen over Devon's county town of Exeter by Dorothy Cole of Exmouth, but in common with the rest of the United Kingdom, it was the years from 1976 onwards that have produced the best UFO sightings and encounters.

Brenda Simpson of Weston-Super-Mare reports more UFO interest in our military aviation on 22nd July 1976:

> "This evening, whilst returning to our home from Banwell direction towards Weston, we were admiring the pretty evening sky. There were a few rosy streaky clouds about and while we were directly opposite the Locking Air Force gates, and looking at the sky, an iridescent orange 'cloud' suddenly appeared. I stress suddenly. My husband, myself and two children; all said, 'Look at that', and my husband stopped the car. This was 9.10 p.m.

"We watched altogether until 9:25 p.m. and during this time five separate streaks appeared, each one slightly longer than the last with a short break between them. The last one completed its formation and we waited for another to appear but instead, a brilliant point of light appeared above the last streak and arced over to the right until it was over the first formation. It suddenly disappeared. We could tell no shape, it just appeared as a point of light. To me it increased and decreased its intensity, but not to the others. It disappeared instantly and all that remained were the streaks, which were fading slightly. They were each double (two parallel streaks of each of the five) in formation. Looking towards Weston it was over Wharl Hill and in total length from the quarry to the golf course (approx.).

"We felt astounded at what we had seen and when finally we decided to carry on our journey my son said, 'Was it from outer space?' This is exactly what my husband, older son and myself were thinking, but did not voice in front of the little one, or even admit out loud. Whilst we have both wondered if people who reported UFOs were cranks or had high and vivid imaginations, we kept fairly open minds. Now, however, we are positive, no doubts at all, that we saw what to us was a UFO. It could have been no plane with the twin trail, colour of the trail; not a cloud because of its quick formation and straight line; not a contrail because it was broken. Nor can we find any possible explanation for the arcing light and its disappearance. In fact, although we were just admiring the view we were all immediately of the same opinion as to what we saw. UFOs were the last thought in our heads. I hope this letter finds you. We are sensible, ordinary, office workers and parents and we don't have vivid imaginations."

On 12th 0ctober 1976, Ed Harris writes of perhaps his closest encounter during his long hours of dedicated skywatching:

"Picture the scene if you can, as I sit on my bed looking out of the open window at the late summer sky. Ursa Major was in full view, unchanged for thousands of years and as I gazed at it I focused on Eta, following the imaginary pointer line to Arcturus, the mighty star in the Bootes group called the Herdsman. This particular constellation holds much fascination for me as I remember studying the star messages emitting from the region of Epsilon (Izar) in my twenties.

"It was one of those times when you begin to wonder at the credibility of it all when almost subconsciously I became aware of a star shining to the left of my vision! I turned my attention towards it trying to pinpoint it in the star field, but to my amazement I found it to be moving across the heavens!

"My binoculars to hand, I focused them on the faintly yellow object as it traversed Polaris, coming to rest a little below Cassiopeia. Here it remained for something like ten minutes, long enough for me to view it through my three-inch refractor. The sight I had took my breath away and in my haste I almost knocked my telescope over! For there in my eyepiece sat a perfect example of a UFO, circular, with raised roof. I watched fascinated, as it seemed to revolve on its own axis, the yellow light turning to light orange in the process.

"Increasing the magnification to X120, I found that it more than filled my field of view, the reason being it was descending! I hurriedly forsook my three-inch and rushed out, armed with the binoculars, just in time to see the strange craft hovering no more than 200 metres above me,

"So as to obtain a better view, I lay on the grass with the optics to my eyes, and as I ranged over the now intensely close vehicle my whole body seemed to relax, and a feeling of complete contentment passed over me; in fact, I had a struggle to stay awake! Was some force at work trying to lull me into a sense of unreality - or was this how we (our race) are meant to be?

> Would we be in a better position to receive our extra-terrestrial hosts if all the bustle and greed of our modern civilisation were forsaken? I, for one, am beginning to wonder, for although having studied Ufology and psychical phenomena for a good many years, I was surprised and unprepared for that feeling of (I call it) being at one with the heavens and it was with heartfelt regret that I witnessed before my eyes the complete disappearance of the craft some five minutes later..."

Thank you, Ed, for putting into words those vital impressions which are so often left out of other UFO reports and which are something which only the experience itself can communicate.

Again at Chard, Somerset, 55-year old Miss Margaret Joy related how she was inspected by some strange alien machine for half-an-hour as it shone a brilliant beam of light into her bedroom.

> "The object was floating above a hedge about 200-feet away. There was no sound and it was all very uncanny. The light seemed to be wandering about and several times fell right across my face. Beneath the light I could see two metal legs which stood out like an upside down 'V'"

The extra-terrestrial Peeping Tom returned with a repeat performance a few nights later, and other people in the area reported the curious object to the local police.

Together with the other previous regional chapters, the amount of strange information contained therein proves beyond doubt that Britain is one of the most prolific sources of UFO sightings and associated phenomena. But so far we have only examined the grassroots material, the individual sightings and reports upon which the UFO mythology, factual or fanciful, has grown. I trust you will forgive me for leaving much of the dialogue in as an original form as possible, for I think it is important that the reader has the opportunity to perceive how the witnesses felt and recorded their strange encounters in an uncomplicated way without the confusing exaggeration or interpretation of their visions by second-hand reporting.

Not that I am implying that the subject under study does not constitute a very solid reality; but in the remaining chapters we are concerned more with the interpretation of the data that I have set out in these first regional collections. For it is in the wider picture, the overall design, that we may find some answers to the mysterious UFOs, which have been seen throughout the length and breadth of the UK.

Chapter 8: UFO Cults and Societies

Sometimes of as much interest as the UFOs are the people engaged in their investigation and the various followings who have turned the subject into a lively, technological and quasi-religious cult. These range from the straight-forward documentation and scientific approach to prophesies of the second coming of Jesus Christ.

Wherever a UFO 'flap' breaks out, the various buffs immediately appear, each giving their own interpretation of the observed facts. How much credence and consideration can be allowed to each individual school of thought is an important issue, as it is usually a spokesman from one or other of the committed societies who appears on the media telling the general public what to think, as if it was a matter of accepted fact. Hence, an impartial look at the bias present in these arguments is useful to determine the degree of predetermination of conclusion inherent in these fixed outlooks.

Perhaps the most predictable opinion will be that offered by an 'expert on astrophysics' or indeed any other vaguely related scientific discipline financed heavily by government funds. The explanation from such a source will simply be that the UFO has been 'identified' or at the very least, explained away.

Any explanation will do so long as it could by some stretch of the imagination fit the facts. The planet Venus is a favourite, as apparently this heavenly body goes on manoeuvres every year, and keen-eyed observers have seen it flying at about 200-feet over Devon, while on other occasions it has been officially 'identified' when in fact the planet was on the other side of the Earth and below the witness's horizon. Of course, if it suits the 'explanation' then the whole solar system will turn on its axis. I recall King Canute faced a similar battle of faith in the powers of the administration some centuries ago when it was thought that the tides were subservient to the power of Kings.

This is not to say that some UFO reports are simply misidentifications. Such bodies as the British Unidentified Flying Object Research Association (2018: Now known as Bufora) attempt to sort the wheat from the chaff, while the largest United Kingdom UFO society, Contact International UFO Research seems uncertain of its exact role. It says of itself:

'Contact International is not a cult, nor even a research unit that adheres strictly to a particular viewpoint. Its policy is one of constant flexibility. It endeavours to approach the UFO riddle with open minded curiosity, progressive thought and properly placed speculation. But above all it undertakes a continuous programme of objective research.'

If, however, it has failed to find a clear viewpoint on what UFOs are, at least it is certain of what its society constitutes:

'Contact International is a non-profit-making organisation; incidentally with branches in 37 different countries, financed from subscriptions and donations. It is run by responsible, intelligent individuals; variously qualified and coming from all walks of life. Each is prepared to devote their free time towards the unravelling of the UFO problem, and as such do not get paid for their efforts.'

With such eminent principles it appears to follow in the tradition of the great British amateur.

It is unfortunate that with most serious UFO research organisations what passes for research is simply the endless filing of thousands upon thousands of observations reportedly there are over 100,000 on record since 1945.

More ambitious advocates talk of processing the data through computers to find, as if by the magic of modern technology, the common denominators that researchers have either failed to notice for the past 30-odd years, or have obscured in the sea of endless flight path coordinates which still defy analysis. One French writer, Aimé Michel, did however show that UFOs appear in regular patterns, apparently being dropped from cigar-shaped craft and radiating on points of the compass to a given distance, then returning to the central craft and in the process, surveying a circular area of several hundred square miles.

Despite this one breakthrough, the conventional investigators of unidentified flying objects seem content to try to prove the reality of the phenomenon to science or governments, which by the standards of their own discipline is impossible until you can get one inside a test-tube.

The US National Aeronautics and Space Administration admitted, in reply to a request from President Carter during his term in office, for their views on the UFO situation, "There is an absence of tangible or physical evidence available for thorough laboratory analysis."

The limitations of this viewpoint are rather like confining evidence in a court of law only to that which could be offered by a forensic expert and ignoring all the eyewitnesses.

We have already seen that 99% of the evidence for the reality of the UFO is observational and not physical, so no wonder that 70 years on from the start of the flying saucer era, science still cannot admit to the subject being worthy of its attentions.

In total contrast, let us look at the other end of the spectrum, expressed to some extent in this letter from a West Country resident:

> "One summer evening in 1975, I was out in my garden and it was getting dark. Looking up towards Rode village I saw one of our bright planets beginning to show up and said to myself, 'I suppose that is Jupiter or Neptune'. Then I looked towards the south-east to see Mars when I noticed moving

from the south at a great height, what looked like a moving star. As it came overhead, I could see it was an amber-yellow coloured bubble, with darker amber colour on its outside. I could see right through.it just like a large bubble. It appeared to be up 10 miles or 100 miles or even 200 miles and must have been very large, and moving steady at a high speed to the north. It took about a minute to fly from south to north. It made no sound. It was not a balloon, or meteorite, as I have seen both at times. It was just a great bubble.

"I have never seen anything like it before and I am sure it could not be a satellite unless it was some new kind. It did not spin, just moved. I did not feel surprised, I have seen many more strange events that could not have been anything of this world, since I was a boy in South America, up to recent times, that have made me become a Christian. I believe we are on the fringe of great events that will be the greatest since Jesus Christ came on this Earth and then ascended to heaven."

Our friend is certainly not alone in his view that the coming of the flying saucers heralds great changes for mankind.

Many have claimed to have had contact with space people and although some reports have clear sincerity, others reveal a distinctly 'human' philosophy and ambition.

One such 'space messenger' offers utopia in exchange for material sacrifice:

> "We have been grading mankind according to spiritual standards, and we know the first ones who will be taken when the space lift-off starts. It will be they who show forth divine qualities. God's chosen ones will be lifted off first and they are God's chosen because they first chose God in preference to any material consideration. They knew the difference between worldly treasures and heavenly treasures."

Perhaps our 'contact' in this case should consider that all mankind is going to be here on Earth for the foreseeable future and that running away to some fairyland in the sky is no solution to hard problems.

However, the 'saving of the chosen few' legend persists very strongly in the psychology of man as a panacea for worldly ills, now or in the future. Even more divine perks are claimed by George King, founder of the Aetherius Society, the largest UFO 'cult' in the UK.

According to King, who died in 1997, the seal was set upon his ministry by none other than Jesus Christ himself on 19th January 1959 with the words: 'We bring to thee this offering in great love and humility from our beloved brother of earth - George -the one whom thou didst choose to be a leader among men of earth in this their new age.'

The Aetherius Society claim to be in contact with Venus and Mars and output a barrage of material from their 'space brothers' that looks suspiciously like various popular practices gleaned from Eastern religions and philosophy, none of which I find distasteful or in any way disapprove. However, the origin of the material seems a little questionable as does the inevitable monopoly on the cosmic telephone line.

This need in contactees to be the only chosen channel for the 'higher beings' bar none is a worrying factor in their credibility. It seems to me that the need for exclusive rights on communications with spiritual beings of great humility is a contradiction in term. It tends to cloud and confuse the cases of apparently genuine experiences with extra-terrestrials, which have, I am convinced, taken place.

However, the mystical relationships people see between UFOs, ley lines and ancient civilisations are very real, as expressed by Janette Chew of Kent:

> "Recently, I came across a copy of Women in which I read of your interest in the network of ley lines across the country. Not sure how to join the lines, I bought a map of SE England and started joining stone circles and earthworks. I obtained not a grid, but an apparently meaningless mass of interlocking triangles. Then the other day I started to read '*The Secret Power of Pyramids*' by Bill Schul and Ed Pettit who have been researching an unknown force field generated within the Great Pyramid and also home-made scaled down versions

with the alignments. Some effects were quicker healing of wounds and illness, dehydration and preservation of foodstuffs, greater relaxation from meditation within a pyramid. Research is not concluded but pyramid, spherical and cone shapes were reckoned to be beneficial to most life forms.

"Going back to my map of triangles, I thought, what if at one time the world was so covered with a vast network of these shapes tapping the magnetism within the Earth, the Earth's magnetic field, forces maybe emanating from space, and the still-disputed fact that the stars and planets influence our actions. Light beams and rays from this source, being built up and stored and modified so that only beneficial influences were received by the people. Therefore, within this network was obtained a limitless supply of energy, for heating, light, machinery, aerial craft, etc. plus for people, animals, plant-life: longevity, freedom from disease, retention of youthfulness, peace of mind, and no urge to make war, (perhaps the Golden Age so often spoken of in ancient writings).

"Are the stones and mounds the remnants of such a structure? Some scientists are said to have taken infrared photographs of Stonehenge and picked up blue outlines meaning the stones are still charged with some kind of energy. Maybe then aerial craft with equipment able to pick up the grid pattern, and with a map of the same with cities marked, used the network as a navigation aid and to recharge power at certain points. If then, this energy is still present, could not such a network be reconstructed for the benefit of mankind? As certain tones notes are also said to be good influences, could this not explain some 'singing stone' legends, also the 'celestial choirs' of John Michell's, *The New Jerusalem?* One marvels at the knowledge of the ancients."

Are Janette's theories just wishful thinking or is there some element of truth in her ideas?

Another popular hypothesis is the, 'We came from elsewhere' school of thought, put forward, for example, by my colleague Ed Harris writing in the UFO magazine, Fountain Journal in 1977:

"There are many subjects that man puzzles over in his attempt to gain knowledge, but the one which poses the most fascinating problems relates to 'Where do we come from and what useful purpose can we serve in our few years upon this earth?' These questions have teased man's imagination since he was first lifted above his near relatives, the apes! There is no way in which an absolute answer can be given either for or against our connection with these simian relations, though if a little of our present day knowledge is applied we can reach some pretty startling answers!

"However hard man tries and he does with intenseness, he cannot get a reasonable degree of intelligent response from these 'ancestors' of ours. Tests, which wouldn't baffle a six-month-old baby, still fail to be solved by these experimental chimps There is a vital spark missing, the speck of independent thought which sets man apart from every other animal species which resides upon this planet. Now, I can already hear the indignant replies that 'We have had time to develop'. Rubbish. Apes have been around for a far sight longer than we have and up to the present time, their evolution is far more advanced than ours! Perhaps we are indeed related to them, but something happened to man many thousands of years ago, which brought him to the level of development which we have reached today.

"What of the theory that we were selected and fostered for a time by extra-terrestrial beings? It's not such a cuckoo idea as it sounds. Why shouldn't an intelligence have visited our planet all those years ago? The fact that we have only recently taken the leap into the skies with our feeble first attempts at space flight are nothing to go by; after all, our so-called science is still in its cradle.

"In some of the old scriptures there are

descriptions of various attempts to colonise and interbreed with early man. How old are these writings and perhaps more importantly, how far back do they refer to and what was it that interbred with man? According to the old writings these beings were referred to as 'gods'. This term to describe them is to be expected and too much emphasis on the word 'god' should be avoided. 'Other beings' would be a more apt word for them, for though they resembled us in many ways, there were some in which they differed considerably.

"Their size was the main factor which shows in the writings, they towered above man (in the days when there were giants upon the face of the earth) and some of them, at least, possessed six fingers. Some- of the so-called experts state blandly that if they existed at all they were no more than mutants.

"Firstly, let us take the query as to whether they existed or not. When the old books were written, the few people capable of recording things were not in the habit of putting down information that wasn't there. In other words, they didn't invent stories just for the sake of things. Their purpose was to chronicle and record the history and legends of their race, not to invent fiction, that is a modern day characteristic. Secondly, about the mutants. It should be realised that if anyone is mutant it is us. Looking back over the scriptures, we will record in our mind what was said about interbreeding with man, trying to breed good points into him and to rid us of our bad ones, in those days we had plenty too. We are the results of artificial breeding, the better amongst us having been selected to carry on our race, while the less successful were destroyed (a point we should bear in mind today perhaps!).

"What happened to these giants of the olden times? According to what was written at the time, they simply vanished from the face of the Earth, in much the same way as the Sumerian race suddenly seemed to appear upon the face of the Earth with their very advanced cultures! Are there perhaps some connections between these ancient giants and the modern day UFO sightings that take place? No one knows where these 'saucers' come from. Some say from outer space, while others think they may come from this planet, from the 'hole' that has been photographed at the North Pole, etc. Wherever they appear from though, serious study of them is needed. At present only cursory attention is applied to solving this, when what is really needed is full scale co-operation between scientists and laymen alike. We get simply nowhere by just reporting sightings, in fact the outcome of our report is fairly obvious to the regular ufologist, a negative response will be given.

"Amongst the old written texts lies enough material to furnish us with more proof than we need that there were superior beings on this Earth many thousands of years ago. It now rests with us whether or not we're willing to believe what we read. The head buried-in-the-sand attitude has gone on long enough, a view, which is encouraged by government and churches alike, so enabling them to better their own ends! People say, 'but what can we do about it?' We must use every day what we can at our disposal to bring to the attention of the public at large the unexplained mysteries of the past and present.

"We put MPs in Parliament, so why not start with them? What they think of us is irrelevant as it's their job to see to our demands! Anyway, some of the subjects, which are discussed in the Commons are a lot more far-fetched than the UFO topic. Stand up and be counted should be the call, and don't be afraid of what others will think of you if they find out you're interested in UFOs. That's a failing of our modern-day society and one that should be dropped immediately for a more sensible one. We can learn a lot from the old writings, perhaps enough to enable us to set ourselves on the road to a better society instead of the one that we tread at present, which is leading us nowhere save to a hasty self-destruction!"

The not unjustified fears about the future of mankind are another common denominator among UFO buffs, spurred on by similar 'messages' from the heavenly host in their chariots of Von Däniken fame.

There is also a tremendous interest in the ancient mysteries and the complex of old straight tracks which criss-cross southern England. Enthusiasts even have their own magazine, The Ley Hunter, devoted to their discovery and analysis.

Wiltshire holds a continuous fascination for its mystic centres and megalithic grandeur. The continued publicity which the area attracts has made it a 'Mecca of Ufology', with thousands of people over the years making an almost religious pilgrimage to this part of ancient Wessex, some just in idle curiosity, some engaged in serious research and others attracted by the area's romantic, almost mystical, atmosphere.

It is not unusual to find up to a hundred devoted sky-watchers sitting on the hills around Warminster on fine Saturday nights during the summer months.

In 1976, this interest gave rise to a centre for UFO studies being established in the town, to provide a long-felt need for all who are genuinely interested in the existence of flying phenomena in local skies, which constitute an aerial enigma throughout our planet.

Although the research groups were misunderstood

by some as commercial ventures encouraging a kind of esoteric tourism, others hotly defended the trend with letters in the local press, including this one from the president of the Hampstead H. G. Wells society:

> "I read with interest the letter from Ken Rogers published in the Journal a few weeks ago in connection with the 'Warminster Thing'. On a recent visit to Warminster, I found that local people had become more aware of the phenomenon. There seemed to be fresh interest more versatile than at any time before. Local groups have set themselves the task of revealing to the world their findings in support of their claim to the existence of UFOs, and whilst this is not a new thing, it is refreshing to a find these groups taking a more practical approach. One group appeared to show not only an interest in the scientific study of the 'Warminster Thing', but in creative pursuits such as yoga, palmistry and astrology. Now there are few small towns, in Britain that can speak of such groups, in which one finds aware, sensible and mature young people.
>
> "I therefore conclude that the 'Warminster Thing' has already proved a great advantage to the town, whether recognised or not, and it is perhaps only a matter of time before the advantages are realised and we see that tourist boom Mr Rogers

mentions in his letter. And, of course, the more people there are with an interest in the phenomenon, the closer we may become to solving the mystery."

However, others were more pessimistic about the future expressed in this plea from researcher Ed Harris, writing in the Journal in the summer of 1977:

"Ufology at present is suffering from the 'dead end' syndrome. Everywhere we go (I refer to ufologists like myself), there are innumerable obstacles put in our way. Ministry departments smile faintly when dealing with a sighting as the details are taken down for investigation, as well they might! For the outcome is a foregone conclusion. Officially there is no such thing as a UFO! So, no matter how sympathetic they might appear to be, don't expect any other result than a negative disappointing one.

"The police, when notified of a sighting, at least appear to do something. Indeed, many police officers themselves have seen UFOs, so what else can they do? If the sighting is local, then the police will look into it, after which they pass the information given on to the Ministry, so getting back to square one! The main thing that comes out of all this is that all information given is taken down and filed. How many thousands of such sightings are there up to the present day?

Even at 20 sightings per week (a very moderate estimate) it amounts to a sizeable sum over 30 years (as of 1980) since major sightings have taken place, and this is only in the UK.

"In the USA, the situation is much more dramatic. Many, many more sightings have been reported, but the administration clamps down on them immediately. Admittedly, they did have an official investigation into UFOs, but it was eventually wound down by saying that no evidence for UFOs had been found. Now there is no official body interested in the subject, or is there? On the surface at least all is still, but they seem to be as keen as ever to receive news of sightings, and this applies to all countries. If they don't now investigate sightings and are confident there are no such things as UFOs, why do they still want reports?

"Many conclusions have been reached, not least of all the one that not officially, but privately, they do believe in UFOs! Perhaps they know a lot more than they let on, perhaps they themselves have first-hand evidence of sightings, or even contact with UFOs. When the Condon report came out some years ago, there was a lot of hot air expounded and many misquotes given (deliberate or otherwise) to disclaim this 1,000-page report, the contents of which I am not going into here. Withholding and concealing evidence is at least a serious scandal in any other field. Why then can ministries get away with it in this sphere? Mainly because ordinary people don't want to get involved with what is to most of them, a topic which marks one as 'odd'.

"One way in which we can help is to report all our sightings etc. to a reputable, non-establishment organisation. Also keep our own records. Write down what has been seen as soon as possible after the event has happened, better still, get it on tape too. Another thing I suggest is to always carry a camera with you in the car. How many sightings have been made in such circumstances, and what a difference a supporting photograph would have made! If more than one person sees something, each write down their accounts separately without first discussing it, first impressions can be changed drastically by talking over the facts.

"This is one area of science—and it is most certainly a science—as future years will show, where the ordinary people hold the key to breaking the UFO code. By our full-time investigations and occasional reports received, even if a person only sees something once in their life, it is still vital evidence needed to go towards the completion. Publicity is always given momentarily to outstanding sightings but how soon is it before it's all forgotten by the public? I wonder how many remember the Scoriton affair now? Information is needed! Descriptions of sightings, crafts, etc. and perhaps most of all, photographs. Armed with these things we can face up to official attitudes with confidence and demand open investigations and files on reports. Without them, things are going to go on as they have done for the last 30 years (as of 1980)! It's up to you! By your help alone can the fascinating mystery before us be solved and the veil of ignorance lifted!"

Perhaps the ultimate danger to the eventual solution of the UFO mystery is contained in this little story from Mr K. Bergin of Croydon:

"I have been interested in UFOs for many years and have learnt to differentiate between genuine UFOs and other phenomena. I have seen various types, but the finest of all was in 1970. I was at Wooton-under-Edge near Bristol, a dull evening with some low cloud. A school football match had finished and myself and another chap were sitting on the grass enjoying the country view.

"It came slowly at approximately 300-400-feet-high. The classical saucer, dome with portholes. The portholes were dimming up and down regularly. Not a sound as it passed overhead and partially disappeared in the cloud. We could still see the lights oscillating a long way off. That week the newspapers reported various sightings. I have, also from this location, seen the huge (red glow) type the size of a bus; and a perfect 26-second view of a greyish-black sphere at 1,000 feet flying fast in daylight. I was driving home half-a-mile away when I saw it. Another man in the street said, 'Christ, what the Hell is it!' I told him but he seemed disinterested and walked off."

Chapter 9: Why The 'Cover-Up'?

Could the high echelons of governments worldwide be so ill informed in these days of radar, satellites, micro-waves and lightning communications, for it to be possible for unidentified aerial craft to cavort about the skies of the British Isles completely unnoticed? It seems unlikely. Indeed, what hidden intrigue must lie behind the interest of world governments, both super powers and small nations, in UFOs. The American, British, and Soviet administrations have all examined the problem in as much detail as diplomacy permits. All of them while verbally stating a nonchalant disinterest are in fact engaged in research programmes.

Speculating in an article for Playboy magazine, Dr J. Alien Hynek, former government adviser to the United States on UFOs states:

" *'Russians solve UFO mystery'*. For years I have opened the New York Times with the fear skittering around the back of my mind that I might find that quote. In my occasional dreams, the story under the headline explains that the Russians have found some previously unthought-of, unstartling explanation for unidentified flying objects. Or worse, that they have made first contact with an alien civilisation conducting reconnaissance missions to our planet. Either story would shake America so hard that the launching of Sputnik in 1957 would appear in retrospect as important as a Russian announcement of a particularly large wheat crop."

Recent leaks indicate that an intensive effort, even a race, is already under way behind the 'Iron curtain' (circa 1980) to achieve that very goal.

The debate in the United Kingdom was given recent and serious consideration in the House of Lords when Lord Clancerty, presented further evidence of the UFO 'cover up'. Previous to this on 27th November 1978, the United Nations 35th Meeting of the Special Political Committee had extensively discussed the phenomenon of UFOs.

The debate had been opened by Sir Eric Gairy, Prime Minister of the Caribbean island state of Grenada. He referred to a recent case of the disappearance of a Cessna light aircraft and its pilot en route to Tasmania, after the apparent aerial abduction of both pilot and plane by a huge cigar-shaped UFO that the alarmed airman had described over the radio before his messages to the air traffic controllers abruptly ceased.

The draft resolution proposed by Grenada read:

> The General Assembly, Mindful of its commitment to promote international cooperation in solving international problems:

Noting the statements made by Grenada at the thirtieth, thirty-first, thirty-second and thirty-third sessions of the General Assembly regarding Unidentified Flying Objects and related phenomena which continue to baffle mankind, and Grenada's appeal to have the United Nations conduct and coordinate research into these baffling phenomena, and to disseminate more widely among the nations of the world information and other data gathered and available on the phenomena:

Aware of the growing interest taken by the people of the world in Unidentified Flying Objects and related phenomena and also interest in strange happenings in various parts of the world, and recognising the commitment to research into these phenomena demonstrated by certain national governments, individual scientists, researchers and educational institutions:

1. Recommends that, in consultation with the appropriate specialised agencies, the United Nations Organisations initiate, conduct and coordinate research into the nature and origin of Unidentified Flying Objects and related phenomena:

2. Requests the Secretary General to invite Member States, specialised agencies and non-governmental organisations to transmit to him by 31st May 1979 information and proposals which would facilitate the

proposed study:

3. Further requests the Secretary General to appoint at the earliest possible date a three-member group of experts under the aegis of the Committee on the Peaceful Uses of Outer Space to study information and proposals submitted to the Secretary-General by Member States, specialised agencies and non-governmental organisations (NGOs).

4. Also decides that the group of experts reports on its work through the Committee on the Peaceful Uses of Outer Space to the thirty fourth session of the General Assembly;

5. Decides further to include in the provisional agenda of the 34th session of the General Assembly an item entitled 'Report of the group of experts of the Committee on the Peaceful Uses of Outer Space for the defining of guidelines for the study of Unidentified Flying Objects and related phenomena.

The Grenada delegation was backed up by the American expert on UFOs, Dr Hynek, together with Lieut. Col L. Coyne who described a close encounter he had while in command of a US Army helicopter. Further evidence was presented by Mr Wellington Friday, Education Minister of Grenada, and Dr Jacques Vallee from France. Vallee is the author of two books on UFOs, 'Anatomy of a

Phenomenon' (1965), and 'Passport to Magonia' (1970), both published in the United Kingdom by Tandem Publishing Ltd.

Friday and Vallee made the following statement to the Special Political Committee:

> Mr Chairman, in the process of science it is common for old human ideas to be challenged by new facts. New knowledge is born of this challenge.
>
> In the process of social development, it is common for new knowledge to trigger emotional reactions with far reaching cultural and political effects. New beliefs are born of this confrontation.
>
> The frequent reporting of unexplained phenomena in the sky of many countries over the last thirty years (as of 1980) presents an opportunity to observe both these processes.
>
> In the documents circulated prior to this meeting, and in preliminary discussions with Mr Kurt Waldheim and representatives of the Outer Space Affairs Group, the essential facts of the phenomenon have been stated by Dr J. Allen Hynek, by Dr Claude Poher and myself. Accordingly, I will limit my remarks to one aspect of the phenomenon, which touches directly on the role of your committee.
>
> To be specific, I would like to call your attention to a new social movement based

on the expectation of contact with beings from outer space. This belief, in many ways, is an emotional one. Although the UFO phenomenon is real and appears to be caused by an unknown physical stimulus, I have so far failed to discover any evidence that it represented the arrival of visitors from outer space.

Instead it is my conclusion, Mr Chairman, that this phenomenon has three aspects:

The first aspect is a physical manifestation that can and should be investigated through already available scientific equipment. Dr Claude Poher, in his recently concluded study sponsored by an agency of the French Government, has now shown the way in this direction. Recently (1977) the Spanish armed forces have also released their files on cases that had resisted analysis by their experts. There is no lack of physical data and there is no lack of competent scientists who are willing to examine them with an open mind.

The second aspect of the UFO phenomenon is psycho-physiological. Witnesses at the scene exhibit disorientation symptoms, a loss of the sense of time, partial paralysis, or loss of voluntary muscle control, auditory and visual hallucinations, eye complaints ranging from conjunctivitis to temporary blindness, massive psychic reactions and longer term effects such as disturbance of sleep and dream patterns and radical behaviour changes.

I do not believe it is within the province or the budget of the United Nations to address such effects directly, except where the United Nations Organisation can serve its traditional role in disseminating scientific information and facilitating exchanges among scholars.

It is the third aspect of the UFO phenomenon which deserves your full attention here, Mr Chairman. This third aspect is the social belief system, which has been generated in all the nations represented on this committee by the expectation of space visitors. This belief has been nurtured by the lack of serious attention given to genuine reports of UFOs, and it is creating new religious, cultural and political concepts of which social science has taken little notice.

I have spent over fifteen years conducting studies of the reports made through official and unofficial channels in France and in the United States. These analyses have been supported by extensive computer statistics. In addition, I have been in frequent communication with scientists in other parts of the world. The conclusions I have reached regarding the social effects of the UFO phenomenon in the cultures I have studied are the following:

1. The belief in space visitors is independent of the physical reality of the UFO phenomenon. In terms of social science, we might say that something is 'real' if enough people believe in it. The UFO phenomenon has now reached this point. The question of knowing whether or not UFOs are physically 'real' is becoming secondary in the mind of the public.

2. The belief in the imminence of UFO 'contact', is an indication of a widening gap between the public and science. We are beginning to pay the price for the negative and prejudiced attitude with which our scientific institutions have treated sincere witnesses of UFO phenomena. Lack of serious, open minded research in this field has encouraged these witnesses to think that science was incapable of dealing with the phenomena. This attitude has led many people to seek answers outside of the rational pursuit of knowledge to which science is dedicated. Only an open exchange of information on the subject could now correct is dangerous trend.

3. In the absence of serious, unbiased research on the subject, the belief in the imminence of UFO 'contact' undermines the image of man as master of his own destiny. In recent years we have seen many books arguing that the earth had been visited by space travellers in prehistoric

times. Although this theory deserves serious study, it is leading many people to suggest that the great achievements of mankind would have been impossible without celestial intervention: the development of agriculture, the mastery of fire and the bases of civilisation are credited to so-called 'higher beings'. Not only does this idea contradict many archaeological facts; it encourages passive expectation of another visit by friendly space creatures to solve current human problems.

4. The expectation of contact with space visitors promotes the concept of political unification of our planet. Through the belief in space entities, a strong and beautiful yearning for global peace is expressing itself. The UFO phenomenon is providing an outside focus for human emotions. Whether this becomes a factor for positive or negative social change will depend on the way in which these emotions are treated and on the seriousness with which the underlying physical phenomenon is investigated. Such is the challenge before this committee.

Mr Chairman, it is not my role to suggest a specific approach to this complex problem. The scientists with whom I am in contact would welcome an opportunity to share their data and their ideas within any structure that could be made available for this purpose.

All the great nations of the world are represented on this committee. Let us keep in mind that the UFO phenomenon may represent an even greater reality. It is our choice to treat it as a threat or as an opportunity for human knowledge.

The hearing was concluded by a request from the Liberian delegate that the statements of the Grenada delegation should be reproduced *in extenso*, a move which apparently brought an attempt to restrict its publication from the United Kingdom representative, who rose to query the cost to the UN of the reproduction. However, she was told that this was part of the normal work of the General Assembly and the attempt failed.

The United Nations was sufficiently impressed with the evidence—including a letter from former NASA astronaut Gordon Cooper, in which he stated that he believed Earth was being visited by extra-terrestrial space vehicles and their occupants from other worlds—for the Special Political Committee to bring the matter before the 47th meeting of the 33rd General Assembly on 8th December 1978.

The meeting delegates decided to... '...request the Secretary-General to transmit to the Committee on the Peaceful Uses of Outer Space the statements made by the delegation of Grenada on the item concerning unidentified flying objects which was submitted for the agenda by Grenada. The relevant documentation would also be transmitted to the

Outer Space Committee for its consideration.'

Unfortunately, the island of Grenada subsequently suffered a left-wing political coup in which Sir Eric Gairy, who was in New York at the time promoting his UN initiative, was deposed. Hence, it seems that further action at the United Nations could be a long time coming.

On 18th January 1979, the UFO problem was debated in a four-hour exchange in the UK's House of Lords.

Before the debate, the Earl of Clancarty, the principal protagonist of the attempt to break through government secrecy on UFOs, stated his hopes for the outcome of his Parliamentary manoeuvre:

> "I want to get the House of Lords UFO study group going, the same as we have in the House of Lords defence study group under Lord Shinwell and keep it going in front of Parliament.
>
> "I want to get the Minister for Defence to go on the air and say what he knows about UFOs like his counterpart, the French Minister of Defence, did in 1974 and told the French people all about UFOs as far as he knew it. He admitted he didn't know everything. He gave them a lot of information and they didn't all panic and run into the English Channel. It would go a long way towards dispelling the feeling that there is a cover up in this country on the subject of UFOs.

In 1974 the French Defence Minister admitted on television that UFOs existed and that the French authorities are making serious scientific investigations. I will be asking for Mr Mulley to go on television and tell us what is being done about sightings in this country. After all, supposing they made open landings tomorrow? There could be panic, because nobody is prepared.

"I hope to use the debate to point out the phenomenal rise in sightings of UFOs over the past year. In 1977, there were 6,000 sightings reported worldwide. In 1978 the figure was more like 1,000 a month.

"The quality of the witnesses has been very high, too. We have had sightings by pilots, police officers, coastguards, meteorologists and radar operators.

"I shall also be referring to the fact that the authorities in many countries are known to have hushed up many well documented sightings. In the early 1950s the American Central Intelligence Agency instructed the USAF to discredit pilots who reported UFOs. Consequently, American pilots stopped reporting them because they feared their careers would suffer if they told what they had seen.

"There has been similar cover up operations in the USSR. However, France takes a rather independent line on this issue, as on many other things, and they are not trying to cover anything up. I am just asking for Mr Mulley to be as frank as his French counterpart."

The Earl has also seen a UFO himself:

"It was in South Kensington, in 1971, when I was living in an old block of flats which had very large windows. It was at night, about 11 p.m. I had not been drinking. I was standing in the kitchen when I noticed a strange light in the sky, coming at an angle from my left.

"I climbed into the kitchen sink to open the window at the top so I could make sure I wasn't just seeing a reflection. The light was moving in a strange sort of zig zagging fashion. It had an eerie light all round it. There was no flashing light, as there would have been if it was an aircraft. Then it lunged away and went out of sight."

Considerable public interest was aroused by the House of Lords debate and some 60 peers, including two bishops attended, together with a packed Strangers' Gallery. The Earl of Clancarty, better known as Brinsley Le Poer Trench, the author of seven books on the subject, put forward a fairly solid case for the existence of the UFO, citing various classic examples which have occurred over the past 25 years.

He referred to the official French investigation team

headed by Dr Claude Poher, known as GEPAN. Based at Toulouse, it is well funded by the French government 'Centre National d'Etudes Spatiales' and is fed information by the local gendarmerie who investigate cases in the field.

Another piece of powerful ammunition in the Earl's evidence was the recent disclosure of 900 pages of official records, originally classified by the CIA but brought out into the open by a successful court case under the US Freedom of Information Act.

The documents reveal that Minuteman underground missile silos and atom bomb storage compounds in the states of Maine, Michigan and Montana were under close surveillance by unidentified flying objects during the first two weeks of November 1975.

Activity logs kept by the North American Air Defence Command tell how a Captain Thomas O'Brien at Malmstrom Air Force Base, witnessed a craft hovering over the underground weapons silo. Meanwhile, at nearby sites, which together with Malmstrom have several squadrons of Minutemen, ground crew saw other, silent, unidentified craft carrying red and white navigation lights, hover and project a black tubular device at a subterranean missile.

Maintaining the non-hostile activity of the extra-terrestrials, the 68-year-old Earl emphasised:

> "It is we Earthlings that have fired on them. Just suppose the Ufonauts decided to make mass landings tomorrow in this country.

There could well be panic here because our people have not been prepared. It is time that the Government informed our people what it knows about UFOs."

The debate continued with the Earl of Kimberley commenting on the US Air Force 'Project Blue Book', which although ostensibly investigating UFO reports in the USA, only became a public relations exercise not to inform the public before it was finally disbanded.

The only Labour peer to speak, Lord Davies of Leek, said that "... if one human being out of the tens of thousands who allege to have seen these phenomena is telling the truth, then there is a dire need for us to look into the matter... we know that poltergeists exist, we know about their activities. Therefore, do not be so ready to scoff at UFOs..."

The Bishop of Norwich expressed fears that UFOs seemed "...to link with a certain religious subculture which... offers a substitute for the true Catholic religion," while Lord Gladwin referred to a growing human wish to, 'trust in other-worldly intervention."

Lord Rankeillour told the House of Lords about a display of flying saucers witnessed by the entire population of 5,000 at Farmington, New Mexico, and went on:

"That was hardly a weather balloon convention. A greater measure of open government is long overdue, and bringing the UFO saga into the realm of respectability would be one way of achieving this."

The government apparently took the debate very seriously and put in Lord Strabolgi, Deputy Chief Whip in the Lords, to answer with the official line.

His remarks were very predictable, referring to the unlikelihood of travel over the great distances between planets. He ignored mankind's recent achievements in outer space, which would, soon after then, see a Voyager II spacecraft fly by Uranus on 30th January 1986, after only eight and a half years in transit, and went on to 'identify' an off-the-cuff sighting mentioned by Lord Gainford as a 'satellite launcher re-entering the atmosphere'.

Perhaps Lord Strabolgi should get in touch with NORAD. They spend 24-hours a day tracking over 10,638 (1980 data) orbital objects, of which five make a random re-entry per week. A man who can 'identify' objects with such casual skill could be useful or, alternatively, very dangerous.

Here, Strabolgi also wondered why UFOs had not been detected on radar, dismissing the New Zealand sightings filmed from a light plane over the Christmas period of 1978 as probably due to 'natural phenomena'. No one seemed to have told him that the six UFOs reported in the incident had also been recorded by two radar stations, with enough concern for the New Zealand Air Force to be put 'on alert'.

So much for the 'official line'! It would be nice if government policies could reflect a little more the thoughts of that great scientist to whom they owe so much of their present day power, Albert Einstein, when he wrote:

> My religion consists of a humble admiration of the illimitable superior spirit who reveals himself in the slight details we are able to perceive with our frail feeble minds. That deeply emotional conviction of a presence of a superior reasoning power, which is revealed in the incomprehensible Universe, forms my idea of God.
>
> Restricting the body of knowledge to a small group deadens the philosophical spirit of a people and leads to spiritual poverty.
>
> The most beautiful and most profound emotion we can experience is the sensation of the mystical. It is the sower of all true science. He to whom this emotion is a stranger, who can no longer wonder and stand rapt in awe, is as good as dead. To know what is impenetrable to us really exists, manifesting itself as the highest wisdom and the most radiant beauty which our dull faculties can comprehend only in their most primitive forms .... this knowledge, this feeling, is at the centre of true religiousness.
>
> The cosmic religious experience is the strongest and noblest mainspring of scientific research.
>
> I cannot believe that God plays dice with

the world.

CHAPTER 10: INNER OR OUTER SPACE?

That UFOs actually exist seems beyond reasonable doubt. In the previous chapters, their idiosyncrasies and regional variations have been discussed and documented for all to see. In the end, it is up to the individual to interpret these observations and conclude their own theories. In this chapter, various possibilities and probabilities are discussed with regard to the nature and origin of the 'craft'.

In general terms, those who accept that one is dealing with some form of mechanised vehicle operated by intelligences not of our human civilisation, divide into two general camps. On the one hand, there are those who believe that visitors come from distant stars and planets across the vast waste of outer space. On the other, there are those who assert that the alien intelligence comes from a parallel universe. In view of the phenomena observed by the witnesses, it seems probable that the final solution may lie somewhere between these two, apparently contradictory, points of view.

UFOs have been recorded in the history of all earth peoples since time began. They have taken many shapes and have been described in the language of the day, sometimes becoming the basis of legends or folk myths. They have often been given religious meaning as visitations from the 'gods'.

In the universe, there must be thousands of planets supporting life. Many of these evolutionary planets must be far in advance of our own planet and must regard the crossing of space by rockets as backward and primitive. There is evidence that the human race itself may owe some of its beginnings on this planet to 'visitors' from another planet. There is also much evidence that these 'visitors' are still taking a very intense interest in Earth, its people, flora and fauna.

But why are they so cautious about making contact? In answer, let me quote from a letter from Mr J. Addison of London S.E.6:

> "It is my belief that our so-called 'civilisation' is the only reason that these friendly beings will not yet make contact in a general way. I think that our visitors will not impart their knowledge because we would at once use it for material gain or aggressive purposes. There is also no doubt that with such knowledge we would want to invade their worlds and try to impose our primitive ways on them."

Dr John Billingham, the English born head of NASA's Radio Search Project, listening for intelligent life in the universe, also holds some interesting views on beings in our galaxy.

Speaking in 1978 he stated:

"It would be very startling if we were the only intelligent beings in a universe which contains billions and billions of stars and planets. Our own galaxy alone contains some thousand billion stars, probably the same number of planets, so it would only take one in a million of those to have life on it and you already have perhaps a million sites in our own galaxy alone where there is life.

"There is one interesting thing about this whole business, we know nothing about these other civilisations and there is an enormous amount which has to be intelligent guesswork. But we think we do know one thing and that is that the other civilisation, should we detect it, must be very much older than we are, must have passed through the stage we are going through a million years ago, ten million, a hundred million years. Because we have just been born. We are 10-years-old when it comes to an ability to talk to other people across the galaxy."

It is my view that we do not live in a chaotic universe ruled by the law of chance. I also think that mankind is not anywhere near the top of the heap as far as cultured civilisations go in this galaxy and that he is not likely to get there until he comes to a realisation of his considerable faults and limitations.

The measure of the status of a society is more likely to be the level of goodwill between its members than the level of technology. Would not an advanced social structure be one in which you would enjoy the pleasure of living? But the 20th Century has produced a 'clever' society where, if anything, the industrial revolution has given us a pressurised life, but not true happiness.

What, you may ask, has all this to do with UFOs? If they are ice crystals, illusions and such, nothing at all: but some 70 years on from the coining of the term 'flying saucer' we can say (those of us who are honest with ourselves) that we are studying an intelligent, sometimes humorous, sometimes philosophical culture, not geared to the pressure situation which we seem so fond of creating.

This other culture has time; it has patience. I always have a good laugh at the 'hostile' brigade who seem to view any evasive practice by Ufonauts as indicative of an aggressive attitude. It would seem to me that a cursory glance at the record would show 99% of the aggression as being of human origin. There is even a 'Don't let them invade us' camp - about time they went back to their caves and played with their flint axes again.

What the human psychology cannot, and is not encouraged to, understand is the concern of a territorially unambitious society, fearing no one it encounters, because it understands the basic purpose and rules of cosmic living. Many have stated them at different times: 'Love others as you would be loved', 'Forgive them their weaknesses', and 'Keep your eyes and desires on the horizon and not on your feet.' We may not have a perfect society, we may never achieve one, but once we stop trying, our morale is lost.

The important factor that gives us grounds for such optimism in the expectation of life in the galaxy, is that our sun is a third generation star and we know the universe is at least 1.4 x10 to the 10th factor years old. Many of the spent-out white dwarf stars must have been the likely home of solar systems millions of years ago before their hydrogen nuclear fuel became exhausted and their radiant energy dropped to a mere fraction of its former output.

There has been plenty of time for advanced intelligent life-forms to have evolved on the planets of suitable population 'I', main sequence type F and G stars. That is, those with the correct radiant output and mass to allow terrestrially similar planets to form and evolve around them, as opposed to only red hot boulders like Mercury or desolate icy orbs, probably not unlike our outer satellite Pluto. One would expect to find such comparable extremes on planetary bodies orbiting stars whose net luminosity is either too hot or too cold to allow the necessary biological evolution to commence within their solar systems.

On the subject of the likelihood of stars having planets, it has already been established that several stellar bodies wobble enough in their rotation to indicate a considerable mass or masses orbiting them and it seems highly likely that the solar model is repeated widely throughout the universe.

Another carefully considered cause for

encouragement in thinking that we are not alone in space, is the fact that our Sun, a normal type G2 star, lives in a galaxy of the spiral configuration. In these galaxies, stellar bodies of the later population 'I' type have organised themselves by centrifugal force into a flattened disc, leaving most of the more unstable older, population 'II' stellar bodies contained in globular dusters at some considerable distance from the majority of F and G stars in the spiral arms of our Milky Way galaxy.

Hence, we should expect biological life to be far more prevalent around us than, say, in a more amorphous galaxy of apparently consistent star distribution.

However, the question remains that if our present ideas on the evolution of the physical universe are correct, in the course of time and as the present bright stars cool, we could be left with a night sky mainly black, filled mostly with burnt out white dwarfs, red giants and black holes caused by collapsed suns.

In the far reaches of our optical vision. we know there are bodies that contradict our present understanding of the absolute laws of physics. Such anomalies as quasars, pulsars, black holes, white holes and bodies which even appear to radiate more energy than that which could be obtained from the annihilation of their entire mass.

All these inexplicable items, together with the mysteries of the sub-atomic world, demonstrate that our understanding of the workings of space and time still have a long way to go.

Back here on Earth, other discoveries and observed phenomena defy our rational logic. Such people as Jean-Pierre Girard, known as the 'French Uri Geller' have nonplussed university professors and professional illusionist alike.

At the Mons University Institute of Psychology in Belgium, while immobilised inside a 'Faraday cage', Girard managed to cause metal bars to bend and warp. With other laboratory samples, he caused structural changes in the metal crystals, detectable only under the microscope, which would normally require temperatures of upwards of 600° C.

How can the human mind achieve these 'miracles'? What is created or affected by such psychic effects every day in the outside world? Is there a whole range of physics upon which we have hardly stumbled? Could these irrational correlations between the normal and paranormal overlap in the case of the UFO?

Ed Harris speculates in the *Fountain Journal*:

> Although psychical research and Ufology are both baffling subjects in their own right, needing two entirely different approaches, there may be more similarity between them than at first meets the eye. The most obvious of these being that both activities usually take place at night, though this is by no means always the case.
>
> In some instances, there are abnormal magnetic reactions in both UFO sightings

and ghost sightings. As a matter of fact, I have known the needle on a compass behave in exactly the same way for both sightings, going completely haywire and spinning around as if possessed with a will of its own!

More subtly, there is sometimes a strange sensation felt, apart from the initial one of shock or surprise in both cases. This feeling seems to be deep rooted, and may express itself either as a tingling numbness, or a total paralysis of the muscles. Paralysis due to fear has been excluded, as this has been felt by more experienced researchers than myself, all of whom have become somewhat cushioned to such effects.

A good example of the similarity between the two sightings can be shown in a case that happened some years ago. A party of six, including myself, set out one night to visit a possible haunted house. The building itself was no more than a burned out shell, save for two ground floor rooms where we decided to set up our 'base', ranging the equipment carefully around the site. This consisted of two portable tape recorders, four cameras, several thermometers, reels of cotton and two compasses. After everything had been set up to our satisfaction and the cotton played out all over the area, this being, in the main, to rule out any 'foul play', we settled back to wait.

It was an April night and heavy low cloud in the moonless sky. The time synchronized on our watches, showed 01:26. Colin (not his real name), had just returned from checking the recorders, when it became apparent that there was something happening.

Some two hundred yards away stood a small knot of trees and coming from these could be heard a strange sort of ringing noise, almost like empty milk bottles being chinked together. As both recorders had a good amount of tape left on the spools we decided to take one with us and investigate, the other being left running where it was.

However, as we were crossing to the trees, a very strange and frightening - for two of my companions - thing happened. The ringing's changed to a continuous high note, and a dull glow shone out through the trees.

Suddenly a gust of wind sprang up, completely' flattening two of the others, and leaving the rest of us staring in amazement after the thing which had shot over our heads, much too quickly for us to bring the cameras into action. We were left with the impression of a golden ball hurtling at us from the trees, and almost instantly vanishing in the distance beyond!

Was this a UFO? Or was this the ghost of

the house, which we had been told about? One thing, which we discovered afterwards, was that our tape had been rendered completely useless, all of it had somehow been demagnetised! Also the compasses, which had been in our pockets refused to work after that night!

This was when I began to think that perhaps there is some connection between 'ghost' and 'UFOs' and the longer I study cases, the more certain I become that there could well be a strong link between the two.

That inveterate compiler of freakish oddities that seem wholly disconnected from natural phenomena, Charles Fort, said of the worldwide incursions of UFOs:

'I think we are property. I say we belong to something. That once upon a time this earth was a no-man's land; that other worlds explored and colonised here and fought among themselves for possession. But now it is owned by something - and that something owns this earth and all others have been warned off.'

The question is, has that contention between outside forces commenced once again, and is the competition, not for territorial frontiers, but for our minds?

He is not the only chronicler of unknown intelligences to conclude that the aliens may be so at variance with anything we know of, that to try and describe them in language everyone understands is an impossible task. Some speculate that the UFOs are not merely from another world but another type of universe, their laws of chemistry and physics foreign to ours. They can break time and space barriers, travel anywhere in the galaxy by some hyper-dimensional link not yet in the scope of our own scientific horizons and normally remain invisible to our circumscribed vision which stops at the ultra-violet and infra-red.

Some psyche-dominated and spiritual thinkers believe they are pure thought energy forms and can be anywhere at any time they please. The weird corollary is that they can actually appear in physical form when they wish and in this manner have been responsible for nearly all legends of heavenly angels and gods from the skies. Looking at certain UFO testimony in retrospect, some say Ufonauts are totally uninhibited by physical limitations such as bodies.

In 1976, some such contact may apparently have been temporarily established with these adaptable, if unlikely, invisible walkers. It came about through the researches of a small group of devoted experimenters from which a bizarre relationship emerged between the 'aliens' and the 'contactees'.

The story commenced with curious inexplicable noises being recorded on the experimenter's cassette-tape recorder, followed by an apparent surveillance of their activities by their 'extra-terrestrial' counterparts.

Materialisations and dematerialisations occurred. Although initially alarmed, the researchers continued and the contact moved into the psychic area, preferred by the 'aliens' as being more reliable.

Those involved, Kevin Goodman, Colin Rees and Chris Butler, began a three-day sky watch at Warminster on 25th October 1976 at 8 p.m. The conditions were cloudy with occasional patches of mist floating about. No UFOs were seen.

The next morning about 11:30 a.m., Chris and Colin went to Cradle Hill copse, taking with them cameras and a tape recorder. When inside the copse they switched on the recorder and continued to make records of the area. However, when played back, the tape clearly recorded a series of rapid clicking sounds, which had not been audible at the copse. Kevin and Colin went back up there later that day with another recorder. Again the same thing happened.

They checked and found it was a fairly regular pattern. To make certain that it was not interference on the tape they took control recordings, but nothing showed up on these. It was therefore reasonable to assume that it must have been from an outside influence.

The same evening, all three took part in another sky watch. Kevin and Colin went up to the barn at Cradle Hill, the aim being to see if more mysterious sounds would appear on the tape. This time it was decided to leave the recorder running for 10 minutes in complete silence.

The sky watch was again unsuccessful and they returned to play back the tape. This time no clicks were evident but instead there were a series of bumping sounds not apparent at the time of recording.

On Thursday the 28th, Colin and Chris returned to the barn area of the copse and this time a recording of what seemed to be a heart beating was obtained. The atmosphere around was heavy. A return visit to Cradle Hill that night at 7 p.m., found the atmosphere again heavy and all three went to the copse. The heartbeat was again recorded and on the way down back from the copse Kevin, 'felt as if we were being scrutinised'.

When at the white gate, a famous sky-watching location, Colin began to feel uneasy and asked Kevin and Chris to move away for a moment. Colin then felt as if someone was breathing down on him. On starting to move off the hill, they all felt that someone who wanted to talk to them was following. The impression faded when they reached the lights of Warminster.

This time, during control recording, Colin felt as if someone was breathing on him and heartbeats were again recorded, but when Kevin and Chris were near it faded away. As they walked through the grounds of Star House, 'someone' running pushed past Colin causing him to lose his balance. This 'someone' was tall, quite solid and of normal human weight but invisible. If this seems farfetched to you, the three persons concerned still possess the tape recordings as evidence. Could this have been the mysterious Warminster 'night walker', which has been reported for some years, and why do psychic phenomena and ghosts occur at the same locations?

A report from Chris Hardwick, Andy Lee and Soteris Georgiou on 1st November 1976, underlines this curious connection:

> "We had been travelling around Warminster during the day when Chris decided he wanted to take some movie shots of Cradle Hill. We arrived at 4:45 p.m. and were filming the hill and copse for about 45 minutes. At 5:30 p.m. we returned to the car (Austin 1100) to warm up as it was a cold day. After about five minutes, our attention was drawn to a peculiar soft thumping from what appeared to be the roof. We heard seven thumps in succession.
>
> "After a lengthy period of debate and attempting to simulate the thumping we agreed that the noise had originated from the bonnet area of the car body, though there was an element of doubt. We discussed several possible causes, Soteris believing that it was due to car body strain or engine contraction due to cooling. However, the other two members of the party pointed out that the car had already cooled as it had been parked for 45 minutes on the rather windy hill and that day's

motoring had not been excessive anyway. Chris remarked that in the two and a half years he had owned the car, he had never heard anything like it before.

"Later in the evening, around 9.45 p.m., Chris spotted two UFOs while out walking. They were bright star-like objects travelling with tremendous speed, but were out of sight in seconds, before Andy or Soteris managed to see them. However, whilst looking for these, Andy, looking straight up, caught sight of a large round faintly luminous UFO, which was circular and about the size of a small soup bowl at arm's length. It appeared to have the texture of a cloud and seemed to be pure white. Moving very fast it was out of sight in seconds heading towards the Cop Heap area, as had been the others, one after the other. Around fifteen minutes later Chris sighted a third UFO similar to the first, this time coming from the Cop Heap direction."

The strange 'contacts' were not confined to Salisbury Plain near Warminster and the teleporting 'alien' suddenly appeared in one researcher's home on his return to Worcester:

'I am writing this letter to tell you of an interesting and at the time, a very frightening, experience that happened to me in the early hours of Thursday morning. The time was 3:10 a.m. I awoke to find the interior of my room was illuminated by a dullish-red glow. Having not noticed the time, I believed it was dawn.

'I turned on my back (I had previously been lying on my side), as I did so I noticed a middle-aged figure sitting on the edge of my bed. He was dressed in normal clothing, except for one thing: it was a very frosty night and he was wearing only a thin shirt and trousers.

'My first thought was to shout out but it seemed as if I was in a trance and unable to even move my limbs. The person then began, his first words were, "Do not be afraid, brother".

'He then proceeded to give me a lecture on what he termed "the follies of your Cantel". I assumed that "Cantel" was their name for Earth, just as 'Venusians' would have a different name for their world. The man's features were not, at first sight, different from any other middle-aged man. I then noticed that he had a few days' growth of beard, only on the very tip of his chin and nowhere else. I became aware of vivid changes in temperature, first hot then cold. The artificial light was not unlike the glow in a camera dark room, except for the fact that it did not appear to cast any shadows.

'The 'man' continued his 'lecture' on the general theme of life on "Cantel" destroying itself through the use of nuclear weapons and military techniques in destroying an enemy. I also noticed that he kept referring to humans as "his brothers".

'When the 'man' had finished his talk there was a moment's silence in which he stared very hard at me. It seemed that he was probing my mind, for what? Hidden information? The 'man' then slowly disappeared, as did the red glow. The man did not seem strange in any way, but I noticed that he wore on his feet what seemed like a pair of moccasins."

A few weeks later the experience was repeated:

'You may think that half past two in the morning is a funny time to be writing a letter, but I am trying to get all the facts down about a reoccurrence of the 'visit' I had a few week ago.

'It began in the same manner; my room being illuminated by a red glow. Again sitting on my bed as if he belonged there was the same 'man' I had encountered on my earlier experience. Nothing about him had changed; he still wore the same shirt and trousers and still maintained the same stubble on his chin.

'He was thumbing through an old copy of a Bible that I possess. The 'man' gazed at me for a while and then said, "Does this concern the universal spirit of truth, that which you call God?"

'I told him that it was, and at his request, told him as much as I knew about the ideas of God. I was then expecting him to reveal what their idea of God was, but no such reply came. He again sat in silence, staring at the closed book. I felt that I must find out more about him and so I began by asking him his name. He said that he was called "Lenston."

'I asked why he had chosen to speak to me instead of, say, a scientist. His reply was that almost anybody could have been chosen, but it seemed to them that I was typical of Earth people, always fighting for survival.

'There were so many things that I wanted to know, but before I had a chance to ask them the 'man' faded away and as before appeared on the opposite side of the room, looking at my three-and-a-half-inch reflector. The 'man' then disappeared again.

'I sat up, spellbound, waiting for him to appear again, but after sitting up motionless for about 10 minutes, watching the red light diminish, I realised that he would not appear again.

'I then went downstairs to fetch a glass of water, the temperature was back to normal and everything seemed as it was.

'My first thought in the morning was that it

was all a dream, but I soon realised that this was not true, as during fetching the water I remembered stubbing my toe on the stairs which made a pretty big bruise.'

Let me now take you through a series of sessions, to which I was occasionally a witness. They imparted a considerable quantity of detailed information, much of it beyond the scope of the contactees' personal knowledge and highlighting a number of very sensitive danger-spots in our world and technology.

The communication experiments were successful, but did not involve the appearance of 'Lenston' in the room as on previous occasions with Colin. The first experiment resulted in Colin seeing 'Lenston' in his mind, although an attempt to talk to him failed. Kevin did, however, start to pick up the very weak 'voice' and a limited conversation ensued, with myself and others present asking questions. Some of these were answered and some Kevin seemed to have difficulty in translating the 'idea' into English, due partly to the speed at which the answer came. Questions on delicate matters were left unanswered and one felt that a very strict code of conduct on what was discussed and not discussed, was being enforced by the other end of the link. On this occasion, there seemed an absolute veto on information regarding the origin or location of the communication.

Questions were also asked by the other end of the link, specifically on the capacity of human culture to deliver a nuclear weapon outside the sphere of

Earth. Supplementary questions included the half-lives of fall-out products. The voice seemed more interested in acquiring information than giving it. However, a friendly diplomatic atmosphere ensued with détente-type manners being observed by both ends of the link. While this was going on, Colin was experiencing a 3D-colour 'vision' of the Earth, as might be observed from an object in orbit some considerable distance away, but not nearly as far as the moon (reference: NASA photos from Apollo moon missions).

In discussion afterwards, the girl sitting next to Colin stated that at the same time she had also been seeing this 'vision'. As this witness is 16 and something of a sceptic, this corroboration is interesting and obviously not pre-arranged. It was almost as if the 'beam' of the communication was not fine enough to only focus on Colin, but also took in the girl who saw the same picture.

In another, much longer, experiment, caution was still the watch-word with 'Lenston'. This time he opened up a bit more, but still offered diplomatic rebuke on some stock questions. The communication was again via Kevin, Colin only having vision.

This split of communication media between two people is interesting. It was almost like tuning a TV when you can lose the picture but keep the sound or vice-versa. During the sessions I asked questions and advice on a number of issues.

'Lenston' stated that they had formerly made

contact with one other person in Warminster (this person was named, but for diplomatic reasons the name must be omitted here as it was stated that this communication had proved unsatisfactory).

Kevin had the impression that 'Lenston' was talking from somewhere very deep underground, but questioning as to his location met only with a "no comment" on all occasions. 'Lenston' did let slip, however, that he was physically on Earth at that moment. Certainly, his description showed him kitted out more for terrestrial living than floating around outer space. An apology was offered about a number of accidents involving motorists hitting some members of his team some years ago, while they were walking near Warminster. When the drivers stopped and returned to the injured people, they had disappeared. 'Lenston' explained that they could teleport over short distances and were several fields away when the car drivers were looking for them on the road. The 10-strong team, of which he was not the leader, had been inexperienced with vehicles and did not realise they could not stop or avoid them. He made no comment on how many people were involved, but one gathered the team had not been badly hurt.

When questioned on their prime concern about potential dangers on the Earth, 'Lenston' was far more specific and detailed in his information than on matters regarding themselves. The answers were unexpected. He had two main worries at the top of the list.

First, the San Andreas Fault in California. 'Lenston'

made it clear that he knew the Earth very well, was widely travelled and experienced in earthy matters. The San Andreas, which lies to the eastern edge of the Central Pacific Plate where it connects to the North American Plate, is a fault line caused by the two plates sliding against one another. Due to the immense friction generated by this, they do not move smoothly. Though only moving inches per year, they jam together and then jump every so often when the pressure becomes too great. The last time San Andreas jumped big time, it caused the great San Francisco earthquake.

The San Andreas fault, which runs roughly north/south through California, has been the cause of a considerable amount of concern and research over the past few years by the US authorities as it is calculated to be long overdue for a major leap - some think of 14-feet or more - whose shockwaves would bring down a high percentage of buildings and structures in that area. The concern was the inspiration for the film, 'Earthquake.'

According to 'Lenston' the San Andreas is now highly unstable and a major cause for concern. He said it was connected to the (as we wrote it) Mariner Trench' but subsequent research indicates that this meant the 'Mariana Trench', estimated by scientists to be the world's deepest ocean section. It lies just off the US Mariana Islands in the west Pacific between New Guinea and Japan at the western edge of the Central Pacific Plate where it joins a sub-division of the Australian Plate and the Eurasian Plate centred on the Philippines. 'Lenston' intimated that seismic activity in the Mariana Trench, was a direct 'red alert' that the San Andreas was about to jump.

All of this was bad news for the west coast of California.

It's no consolation either for Japan which lies just to the north-western edge of the Central Pacific Plate where earthquakes are about as common as No. 9 buses up Kensington High Street. Also the eastern edge of the Central Pacific Plate runs right up the west coast of Oregon, Washington State, through along British Columbia (Vancouver) Canada, and up into US Alaska. It was at this north-eastern edge, of the Central Pacific Plate that in 1964 the faults let rip and produced the highest Richter scale earthquake readings in recorded history. So large was the Alaska quake that mountains changed altitude. Fortunately, in such a very under-populated area, loss of life was minimal. Although the town of Anchorage suffered damage this would in no way be similar to the havoc caused in California by a quake of comparable dimensions.

*Update note, 2018, On October 17, 1989, nine years after the original publication of this book, San Francisco was struck by a major 6.9 magnitude quake, known as Loma Prieta earthquake. It was the strongest earthquake to hit the area since the 1906 event and caused 63 deaths and an estimated $6 billion in property damage.

Having gone deeply into this number one item of

concern, about which I may add Colin and Kevin had little personal knowledge, 'Lenston' mentioned his number two listing: Biological Warfare. It was not entirely certain from the questions and answers whether this was in isolation, or as connected to the number one earthquake problem.

New developments causing concern are the capacity to interfere with DNA by transplantation of chromosomes and genes. To quote from an excellent piece of research by Plain Truth from Dr Liebe F. Cavalieri, Professor of Biochemistry at Cornell University:

> "A single unrecognised accident could contaminate the entire Earth with an ineradicable and dangerous agent that might not reveal its presence until its deadly work was done. It is possible, intentionally or unintentionally, to construct highly dangerous agents of other types, worse than anything yet envisioned in biological warfare."

Harvard biologist Dr Ruth Hubbard stresses:

> "This [research] is more hazardous than the atom bomb. It could unleash "super-bacteria" that are resistant to drugs and spread new types of disease worldwide."

Dr Robert Sinsheimer, chairman of the Biology Division of the California Institute of Technology, warns that the new genetics may well be irreversible. "Because of human fallibility, these new organisms are almost certain to escape," Dr

Sinsheimer says, "There's no way to recapture them, and thus we have the great potential for a major calamity."

With such a comment from Cal Tech perhaps the concern of 'Lenston' was compounded by the risk of an escape of such superbugs in the event of the chaos caused by a major earthquake affecting California. It is known that quite a number of government facilities are located near the San Andreas Fault. Indeed, some schools, hospitals and even nuclear power stations are built nearly over it.

Update 2018: Of course we are now all-too familiar with the threat from antibiotic-resistant germs, while the recent developments in CRISPR gene editing may well be the very thing 'Lenston' was warning about. In the right hands, gene editing can save lives. In the wrong hands, one can only speculate as to the havoc that could be wreaked by unchecked genetic manipulation.

Further communication from 'Lenston' was reported on 6th May 1977, when the dialogue recorded went as follows:

Kevin: "I'm in a black room. It's all black. Contact is made."
Colin: "Can you speak to Lenston?"
Kevin: "Yes."
Colin: "Does he know what time we are from?"
Kevin/L: "AD 1977 (pause) Please remember he

does not work in base 10."
Colin: "Ask Lenston where you are?"
Kevin/L: "Transition Hall. I am at liberty to tell you about our star system except its location in the universe."
Colin: "They do live on a planet?"
Kevin/L: "Yes!"
Colin: "What kind of a star is it?"
Kevin/L: "Main stage."
Colin: "Any other planets?'
Kevin/L: "Yes, three."
Colin: "Do any have satellites?"
Kevin\L: "No."
Colin: "Is the planet like Earth?"
Kevin/L: "Yes."
Colin: "Do they have a name for the star?"
Kevin/L: "Pentaris."
Colin: "Will they tell us what we call it?"
Kevin/L: "You don't know about it."
Colin: "Do they visit other planets in our solar system?'
Kevin/L: "About six months of your time scale ago."
Colin: "Do they know Earth well?"
Kevin/L: "Yes,"
Colin: "Ask him nicely if they were responsible for the UFO activity in the Worchester area?"
Kevin/L: "They were not."
Colin: "So they were hoaxes?'
Kevin/L: "Not our group."
Nick: "Does he know of any other planets and star systems that contain life?'

Kevin/L: 'In your scale, billions, within a radius of 12 parsecs." (39.12 light years)
Colin: "Does he know of any in our galaxy?"
Kevin/L: "Many."
Colin: "In our solar system?"
Kevin/L: "None."
Colin: "Which is the nearest?"
Kevin/L: "No comment."
Nick: "Do they know of us?"
Kevin/L: "Yes, next question is how, all I can tell you is that your radio signals have reached them."
Nick: "Have they tried to contact us?"
Kevin/L: "Yes."
Colin: "Are they on their way?"
Kevin/L: "They have been and gone."
Nick: "Before man?"
Kevin/L: (With impatience) "They have received your radio signals. They are within 70 light years."
Colin: "They pick up everything?"
Kevin/L: "Your Sci-Fi programmes amuse them."
Colin: "Have they visited any other planets in our system?"
Kevin/L: "Moon, Mars."
Colin: "No other?"
Kevin/L: "No."
Colin: "What is their interest in Mars?"
Kevin/L: "Scientific exploration."
Colin: "The Moon?"
Kevin/L: "I cannot say."
Colin: "What about transport?"

Kevin/L: "Yes, but understand he is not a technician."
Colin: "Do they travel faster than sound?"
Kevin/L: "Sound!"
Colin: "First, I mean..."
Kevin/L: "Of course."
Colin: "Light?"
Kevin/L: "Of course (pause) faster than time."
Colin: "Than time?"
Kevin/L: "You cannot begin to comprehend it."
Colin: "So it takes very little time?"
Kevin/L: "No they' travel so fast that they build up an eddy... They land spiritually before physically. That is why UFOs appear transparent."
Nick: "About the speed of light, is the bit about time an off-spring from about going faster than light?'
Kevin/L: "Not a technician, but we do travel faster than time, but we cannot go from one stream to another."
Colin: "So they live in our time?"
Kevin/L: "Yes, through this medium (telepathy) time and space has no meaning."
Colin: "About Warminster, those UFOs we saw, were they UFOs?"
Kevin/L: "They were UFOs, routine scout mission, they knew you were there, (impatient). You don't understand, in Warminster I told you of the folly of nuclear weapons; the Plain by Warminster, Porton Down and other secret areas are nearby."
Nick: "Do you use nuclear power?"
Kevin/L: "We went beyond that millions of

years ago."
Nick: "Will you contact all the people of Earth?"
Kevin/L: "In time."
Colin: "Near future?"
Kevin/L: "When the people are ready. Ratio of 20 to one do not believe in us. If we landed there would be mass terror, a breakdown of law."
Nick: "Would it have happened if the governments had not covered up the UFOs?"
Kevin/L: "They cannot understand them."
Nick: "What would have happened if they did?"
Kevin/L: "We would have landed years ago."
Nick: "What is your attitude towards us?"
Kevin/L: "We have none, we think you are a small world waiting to be enveloped in the cosmic fold."
Colin: "The other planet, is it in this fold?"
Kevin/L: "Yes."
Nick: "How long ago?"
Kevin/L: "Time has no meaning. Billions of years is nothing in the scale of the universe."
Nick: "Any other barriers to be broken down after time?"
Kevin/L: "Just death."

This different understanding these supposedly advanced civilisations have of time and space, is also reflected in this communication from a different claimed extra-terrestrial origin:

> "All life is a unity. All symbols are multiple. All things repeat in a myriad of

different forms.

"The Earth is a living thing. It has a body which is alive. The energy of its life force is that elusive energy sometimes called Prana, the power behind all biological life.

"In ancient times, the working of this was understood, used and outlined in the earthworks marking the lines of the earth force. This is a mirror reflection of the cosmic forces of the sky and a duplication, in ripple form of the starry heavens and its energies. All points of the surface of the sphere have sympathetic points in the sky and with other points in time and space.

"Vehicles in transit may drop into this time and place, be seen to transit to some other point in your vision and disappear. At this point they have translated to another point in the cosmos, not necessarily very far away, and appear at their new location. Your level has been used for transit, not necessarily for any other reason. The unified field theory of Einstein is worthy of closer inspection in this connection. It is also very advisable to think very carefully before experimentation, as former civilisations have burnt their fingers fooling with this area of cosmic science."

This put me in mind of the alleged 'Philadelphia experiment' in 1943, when a US destroyer, USS Eldridge, was claimed to have disappeared into thin air, reappearing over 200km away, during a military experiment, based on the unified field theory.

But perhaps in daring to venture into this controversial area of psychic communication with peoples of other worlds, we are getting a little out of our depth. However, many writers, and indeed some scientists such as Russell Targ, of Stanford's SRI Laboratory, have speculated that some form of Extra-Sensory Perception (ESP), is the only likely and 'immediate' means available to communicate over light-years of space.

Much of the observed phenomena also leans towards a suggestion of means of transport or translation far beyond our mechanical technology, as for instance in this report from Mr L. G. Warden:

> "We have seen recently a UFO like a fluorescent tube in the south west travelling slowly towards south west in a clear sky and it was travelling against the wind direction."

Stanley T. Richardson of Maidstone also observed another inexplicable 'tube' in 1974. He writes:

> "Some years ago, my wife and I were driving along one evening towards Tunbridge Wells and were out in the country away from any lights that could cause reflections, etc., when suddenly, I saw through my side window, a very intense beam of green light. I can only describe it as a fluorescent tube reaching from the high, broken cloud to the ground.

It lasted a good five or six seconds. I thought, 'You're seeing things' and was prepared to ignore it when I saw my wife looking in the same direction. On impulse I said, 'What's up?' and she replied, 'I have just seen a beam of green light appear!'

"She verified what I had seen, but neither of us could give a rational explanation."

However, apart from these rather Star Trek-like possibilities of 'beaming up', perhaps over only relatively short distances, it would seem that the use of some form of conventional 'ship' must form the foundation for prolonged journeys in space—or so we are led to believe from this account of 'communication' with the aliens:

"The atmosphere was beautiful; it was one of deep calm and intense peace. Each of the persons there knew what they were doing and quietly got on with their work. It was a clean atmosphere, there was no sense of competition or incompetence. They were all working together for the good of the whole community. It is because of their desire to establish communications with more people on this planet that I am writing to you now.

"It would seem that these are the "secret chiefs" of various occult (esoteric) orders and that their communications with us are much more than we would realise.

"Now our main contact is with a vessel orbiting the Earth; this would appear to be a laboratory ship which we have numbered "M89". Here, there are experts in many fields, some of whom I have been privileged to meet and work with, always in this atmosphere of intense calm and gratitude, and great happiness to meet and work together.

"One of the greatest problems I find, is that of closing my mind to the noise of its own thoughts and the concentration of energy in one direction. Since we started, we have been given aids to our concentration, which gives us almost instantaneous contact with these people. I cannot express the joy and gratitude I owe these persons. My only hope is that through this letter more people will try to contact them."

The combined presence of a 'craft' and beams of light was witnessed by Mr Keith Palmer of London, at Wood Green, on 15th August 1966.

The time was 2 a.m. and Mr Palmer saw an object which appeared half the size of the full moon approach from Edmonton. When 150 yards from the house it stopped, hovered and suddenly released two smaller brightly-lit discs. These deployed downward, pointing shafts of pure white light so bright the witness could read his watch; the time was now 2:10 a.m.

The outriders then turned off their searchlights, re-entered the parent craft and flew slowly on over Mr Palmer's house. As it did so, he could clearly distinguish a myriad of small multi-coloured rotating lights underneath the craft and also detected a high-pitched hum.

The following morning, the somewhat shaken witness found he had suffered a sunburn rash on his face and arms, supposedly caused by ultra-violet radiation from this unearthly visitor.

It has been speculated that UFOs surround themselves with a bubble of highly ionised air. In this condition, the component ions take up only about one 10,000th of the space occupied by their parent molecules. The net result is that the disc is flying in a self-created near vacuum, which would substantially cancel out air resistance, prevent sonic boom shockwaves from the leading edges at high speed and cause the air around the UFO to give off the characteristic glow.

The noise of high-tension emission was also heard by Mrs Rostenberg, when she witnessed her amazing UFO sighting in 1954 in Staffordshire:

> "I was getting changed and I heard this terrific noise, it was just like a giant cauldron of water being poured on to a fire, a 'sshhh" sort of noise and my first reaction was 'Oh, the children!'
>
> "I thought it might be a plane crashing or something like that. I slipped my jumper on and went outside to find my two sons lying flat on the ground in front of the house, shouting, 'Mummy, Mummy, there's a flying saucer.' Naturally I said, 'Come on,

don't be stupid, come in the house,' but felt a sort of a strange sensation.

"I worked my way up the side of the house to where we have a pump where we used to get all our water from and automatically looked up to see this - all I can describe as a huge Mexican hat! It was stationary and was bright silver in colour and had a dome. It was tilted so that I could see the occupants in it.

"I saw people in it. There were two people in there. These people were beautiful people. That's the only way I can describe them. They had long golden hair like a pageboy bob, just like the old kings. They had a sort of polo-neck jumper affair, like a ski-top suit in pale blue.

"Now these people weren't sat behind, one behind the other, they were sat together. But this whatever it was, was tilted so that I could see them and they could see me. It had this perspex or glass or whatever it was, they could see and I could see them. They had beautiful faces and I shall never forget their faces as long as I live.

"Their foreheads seemed to be a bit longer than the bottom of their faces than in normal people. But maybe this was due to whatever they had around their heads which was like a transparent fish bowl.

"And I was absolutely paralysed with fear. I

couldn't move although my mind was ticking over. And they looked so sympathetic that I was just mesmerised for what seemed to be ages but it could only have been seconds. I turned to sort of look down at the boys, I was unaware that they were with me because I was so absorbed and the next thing I looked up and it was gone!

"It had been just hovering on top of the roof. The roof had been completely blotted out by this massive object. I assume it went straight up, because for a short while after in the sky I looked around and I said to my boys 'Can you see anything?' and they said, 'There it is, Mum', and they pointed up and I watched it.

"It was just like a little cotton reel in the sky and it circled us three times and then it just shot off, and that was it!

"When I started to analyse myself afterwards, I feared that I might have had an hallucination, but then I knew I hadn't had, because my sons were so sure about what they had seen, and what I'd seen. It went through my mind that it was a secret weapon from Russia and then I thought, 'Well, it can't be that because if they had something like that they wouldn't need to fear anybody or anything!

"When my husband came home from the

office I was locked in the house with my children under a big kitchen table that we were using.

"It's funny now when I look back, it sounds absolutely ridiculous, but this is the truth. This happened and that's it. It was very embarrassing at the time and people, they possibly thought, 'Oh she's a nutter', but who cares? This is something that happened to me, and I'm a practically-minded person and that's it."

So at the end of the day, what aggregate of material have we accumulated in our analysis of the UFO-UK situation?

First, lights in the sky, lights in groups, lights in formation, individual lights, travelling, stopping, undertaking non-ballistic trajectories, reported both by day and by night.

Second, landings of objects both by day and by night, physical objects that leave tangible tracings on the ground, burn marks, impressions, physical damage to buildings seen by multiple numbers of witnesses sometimes at different locations and not in association with each other.

Third, 'spacemen' emerging from the landed craft, undertaking various operations on the ground, re-entering the craft and taking off.

This includes 'humanoids' seen in the area with various non-human characteristics, i.e. physical height, capacity to move by some method of personnel transport built into their equipment. Seen in full spacesuit, seen without their spacesuits and also on occasion talking to bystanders who are alarmed at the inexplicable strangeness of their visitors.

Fourth, disappearance of various cattle without trace, witnessed teleportation of herds, short and intermediate distances.

Fifth, unusual characteristics associated with these same cattle, i.e. bullock to heifer birth ratio altered, unusual low milk yields and strange unnatural behaviour as if they were aware of certain areas in which they dare not go.

Sixth, UFOs seen entering into the sea and on different emerging from the sea. UFOs seen causing a landslide on the coast and the possible implantation of some kind of instrument package.

Seventh, various tangible and witnessed interference, caused in near vicinity of the UFOs, their occupants or locations where they have been seen.

Accepting all of these were reported facts, is there anywhere else but outer space that could cause the originations of these machinations on mankind? Indeed, is space itself as desolate a wasteland as we imagine it? According to Sir Fred Hoyle, space is the very home of life. Speaking in 1978 he stated:

> "Life is so exceedingly complicated that it couldn't have happened on the Earth. One needs all the resources of the universe or of our galaxy, stars and so forth, to put life together.

"We think of the Earth not as a place where life originated, but as a maintenance station for life."

Forty complex biochemical and organic molecules are known to exist in space including cellulose and chlorophyll, and most of the comets are now thought to be composed of water. Indeed, Professor Chandra Wichramasinghe of University College, Cardiff, thinks that much of the Earth's oceanic water came here this way. He and Hoyle have also posited that debris from some comets brought viruses that have caused human and animal pandemics. So why not life in space?

Of the 30 or so stellar bodies that lie within 16.4 light years of us, could not at least one have evolved advanced life forms? Or can we go even further, as some modern parapsychology researchers speculate, that nature knows how to balance itself and has a consciousness of what is happening far beyond strict ABC mechanics.

The scientist and writer, Lyall Watson (1939-2008), who, in 1973 wrote the best-seller, *Supernature* among other books, demonstrated that nature appears to compensate for certain events before they even happen. For example, on occasion predators of a particular species will multiply simultaneously or even just before their food stocks increase. It seems there is a natural environmental 'balance-control' governing genetics and breeding, ever-seeking to maintain the delicate equilibrium of survival and evolution of species and even planets.

Together with numerous experiments indicating that even plants, as well as humans and animals, may have an element of ESP, we are now being led to the inevitable conclusion that the universe is not random; that matter itself is not a random property of lifeless, unthinking particles. That indeed, we are all connected and the one is all part of the whole and the whole could know everything. Is the only limit to our realisation of tomorrow, our doubts of today?

However, the ultimate analysis of the existence of UFOs may not be so important as the overall awareness of our place in the universe.

The poet Archibald McNeish, writing in the New York Times on the occasion of man's first landing on the Moon in Apollo II on 20th July 1969, captured this awareness with these simple words:

For the first time in all of time

Men have seen the Earth.,

Seen it not as continents or oceans

From the little distance of a hundred miles or two

or three.

But seen it from the depths of space,

The medieval notion of the Earth

Put man at the centre of everything,

UFO UK - UPDATED

The nuclear notion of the Earth
Put man nowhere,
Beyond the range of reason,
And lost in absurdity and war,

This latest notion may have other consequences,
It may re-make our image of mankind,
No longer that victim off at the margins of reality
And no longer that preposterous figure at the centre,

To see the Earth as it truly is,
is to see ourselves as riders on the Earth together,
Brothers who know now the truth of this.

Chapter 11: Dead men talk

It is estimated that over the past 15 years, more than 200 UFO researchers have died, some naturally, but some under rather suspicious circumstances.

Without being paranoid, some of the incidents of death tend to follow known patterns of covert assassination, which have been used over the years to make the loss look just like a natural one. In-your-face murders tend to draw public attention, get on the news and also invoke police investigations.

In my undercover career, about which I have written in my autobiography, *Secret Life of a Spook,* I have been tasked to investigate many things that, officially, did not fall into the authorities' domains. They were off-the-books operations, where governments could claim plausible deniability and remain in the shadows, but about which they had an insatiable need to know. Many of these ops remained compartmentalised within the particular commissioning agency, never known about by their respective governments—whether UK or US—as I have worked for both sides of the ditch known as the Atlantic Ocean.

In referring to some of these matters in this chapter, I am steering a path between what is established fact, what seems highly indicated and what I recognise as the established MO (modus operandi). The latter of these was shared with me by people for whom I acted as carer and memoir-censor, after they retired from service. Most of these memoirs they wrote were suppressed or sanitised, and often by me, as they would have provided political capital for national insecurity.

However, the agencies always like to know what one another is doing and why. Who gets to see this data up the line is always a bit of a mystery.

One of the problems with the whole ethos of 'national security' is that it allows much internal concealment from elected politicians, about matters that they don't 'need to know'. Indeed, it fosters internal 'independent groups' who assume the 'right' to make executive decisions that often affect, or even make, history. It is these groups' intention to 'control the controllers' of the official governmental oversight committees whose role is to guide and police these very same agencies. These secretive groups wish to protect the agencies from criticism or indeed from having their wings clipped where they have previously had cart blanche.

So let's take a look at some of the vital and important findings of these lost researchers to see what they were saying that needed to be 'shut up'.

I have not run this in any chronological order and I make no implication or cross-reference between their schools of thought. Just take them one at a time and make up your own mind. Throughout, remember that both 'ET' and the agencies are past masters at deception, obfuscation, smoke and mirrors, and distraction. A lie nested between two truths, or a truth lodged between two lies, is the standard method of confusion; it is only amateurs who engage in outright lies. Perhaps also include politicians in this category, as they're deluded that their 'standing' will allow folk to blindly believe their statements and never more so than today, in 2018!

Let's start with Bill Cooper, who died in 2001, aged 58. You can search online for more details on all these people I will mention, but we know that Bill was murdered by being set up in a situation where he was supposedly resisting arrest for some alleged misdemeanour.

Writer and radio host, Milton William "Bill" Cooper was best known for writing *Behold a Pale Horse*. The book warned of multiple global conspiracies, including extra-terrestrial aliens. The mainstream media described him as, "a wanted militia figure who vowed that he would never be taken alive."

Indeed, he was not. Cooper was shot, having been lured outside of his home. It was claimed that he wounded a sheriff's deputy and was killed in return fire but the inside story is somewhat different to the public domain reports. He had been 'stalked' by a 'kill team' for some days, when he let his guard slip and allowed himself to be drawn out into an exposed situation. As I, on more than one occasion, have been targeted by a kill team myself, I know the techniques. Additionally, as mentioned, I previously took care of retired members of these units who shared their training and lifetime experiences with me over many a cup of coffee or bevvy of alcohol.

Over his lifetime, Cooper had access to a lot of inside intelligence and was blunt and challenging in his public presentations and positively politically incorrect by nature.

In his many revelations, he outlined the involvement of governments in the UFO scene, the total reality of UFOs and indeed the many unethical practices engaged in over the decades to keep the general public (the sheeples) in the dark. As they say of mushrooms, keep them in the dark and throw shit on them constantly and they grow just beautifully. It is a sad compliment to Bill Cooper's data and presentations that someone issued that 'wet team' order for him to be taken out.

An obscure 'kill', in my opinion, was the death by tragic road accident of Eugene Merle 'Gene' Shoemaker (1928–1997). A geologist, Shoemaker was best known for co-discovering the Comet, Shoemaker–Levy 9. He was also the first director of the United States Geological Survey's Astrogeology Research Program.

He died, aged 69, in a head-on car collision in Australia, while on a meteor crater hunting expedition on the remote Tanami Track, a few hundred kilometres northwest of Alice Springs. Shoemaker's wife Carolyn, also an eminent astronomer, survived but was severely injured in the crash. The chances of such an 'accident' occurring on a remote and quiet outback track are slim to say the least, and such 'traffic accidents' are a favourite method of removing 'persons of interest' who have fallen foul of the executive action committees.

Why kill this well respected astronomer? Shoemaker and his wife were the leading NEO (Near Earth Objects) hunters devoting years of their personal time to examining and comparing detailed photos of the star patterns to identify rogue objects moving in space near to the Earth. They were finding out far too much about the traffic going on in our solar neighbourhood, but before they could publish their latest findings they were stopped in the simplest and most brutal way.

Philip 'Phil' Schneider (1947-1996) claimed to be an ex-government structural engineer involved in building deep underground military bases (DUMB) in the USA.

Among Schneider's claims was his involvement in a lethal confrontation with very aggressive grey aliens deep underground at Dulce, while working on the base there.

These claims could be considered extravagant, were it not for his blatant murder by strangulation in his apartment in 1996.

Official records state that, despite missing the index

and middle fingers from his left hand (lost, he said, during the Dulce incident) he committed suicide by strangling himself to death with a knotted rubber catheter tube. Friends questioned why he would have chosen apparent self-strangulation when, in his apartment, he had both medication and firearms that could have done the job much more easily.

The farcical suicide ruling by the coroner came regardless of the fact that for him to have performed the act himself and alone, would have required the skills of Houdini with both hands intact. His ex-wife, Cynthia, also believes he was murdered. She recounts Schneider as saying if he ever 'committed suicide', you would know that he had been murdered.

He gave many public lectures on his experiences in the last few years of his life, which included fleetingly observing aliens processing vats of human body parts to extract enzymes. I cannot totally endorse his claims, but certainly he was saying enough to get him wasted in a very crude and obvious manner. You can find a number of his videoed speeches online.

An academic heavyweight who had to be eliminated was American psychiatrist, Dr John Edward Mack (1929–2004). He was also known as a writer, parapsychologist and held a professorship at Harvard Medical School. He had even won a Pulitzer Prize but it was his research into alien abduction experiences that may have prematurely ended his life.

He had gathered information from many people who said they had been experimented on by aliens aboard their ships. Under hypnosis, they described their experiences of the medical and reproductive procedures they were put through while they were taken. He wrote several books and gave lectures about this work.

Mack was in London on September 27th 2004, to lecture at a T. E. Lawrence Society-sponsored conference, when he was killed by a supposedly drunken driver. He was hit as he walked home alone after a dinner with friends.

It goes without saying that for the op. (although an inquest declared it to be an accident) would likely have been within the domain of British Intelligence Agencies who, at the very least, would have been requested to 'look the other way.' The scene of the 'accident' is a junction of good visibility with pavement protecting bollards running down one side of the road. A very unlikely location for a casual accident?

Dr Karla Turner (1947–1996) was well-known and respected within the UFO world as an alien-abduction researcher. Again, using hypnosis to recover memories, she gathered many detailed witness reports from women who claimed to have been involved in 'hybrid breeding programs'.

Dr Turner exposed the secret undercover investigations by special access units of the US military, in their subsequent interrogation of these abduction targets, sometimes using rather unethical methods such as sodium pentothal 'truth serum'. Through her research, Dr Turner became a key figure in focusing on the dark side of UFO activity, whether extra-terrestrial or man-made, and hence a target for those who would rather she desist from her activities.

Dr Turner died of breast cancer at the age of 48, but one well-used method of 'removing' people is by the induction of various forms of aggressive cancer. This involves the use of a hand-held microwave weapon, which damages DNA and sets the malady in train. Death follows, sometimes months later, from 'natural causes.'

James Vincent Forrestal (1892–1949), was the first US Secretary of Defense. Apparently suffering from depression and exhaustion from overwork, he was being treated as an in-patient at the National Naval Medical Centre in Bethesda, Maryland. Forrestal seemed to be on the road to recovery, but in the early hours of May 22nd, he was said to have 'committed suicide' by launching himself from the 16th floor of his hospital room window, clad only in pyjama bottoms, with a bathrobe cord tied around his neck.

The report into Forrestal's death remained secret until 2004, when it was released as a result of a Freedom of Information request. The report can only be described as lacking curiosity at the strange events immediately prior to his death.

It reveals, but does not follow up, testimony from a

nurse and a photographer, who both saw broken glass, thought to be from a make-shift ashtray, on the bed right after Forrestal was missed at 1:55 a.m. However, just ten minutes before this, he had been observed in a regular check by a Navy medic, as apparently being asleep in bed.

Forrestal had been the subject of a smear campaign in the press and was known as a critic of both communists and Zionists, who were not unknown to 'suicide' their opponents.

However, neither this, nor his knowledge of one of the most famous episodes in UFO history, was investigated. It is the latter that I know was behind his untimely death; one that was most definitely a murder, not a suicide.

Forrestal had been privy to all the data and recovery of the Roswell UFO Crash two years earlier in 1947. He knew about the alien occupants, both dead and alive and he wanted to tell the American public the truth. On the day of his death he was going to be released and his brother was travelling to the hospital to pick him up.

'They' got him just in time, for if such a figure had gone public, we would surely not still be living with official denial in the face of reliable evidence to the contrary of the existence of UFOs. Am I making this up? Not a bit of it; one of my closest friends is a family member of James Forrestal (RIP). One of the bravest men in American history!

These and many others have died in the pursuit of honesty, ethics and the exposure of the truth to the world on the many matters about which you ought to be aware. Many reasons are cited for these terrible acts such as the ubiquitous 'national security', the avoidance of public panic, keeping technical secrets from one's enemies, or defending the State or Realm. The reality is more the selfish need to maintain the status quo, to preserve the advantage for the established family elites who own 90% of this world, and their dubious co-operations with the dark side of aliens in the neighbourhood.

Who you gonna call? There is no one to call. The police are way out of their depth on the subject, or shy away from it. The government ministries don't want to know as they would be told to do something about it, which they are either impotent to do, or are told by the 'Inner Keep' to hold the thin red line.

UFO researchers just file it all away and the serious ones get bumped off. Meanwhile the mainstream media, who on occasion run a story or two (in particular the UK's Daily Express in recent years), but then move on with business as usual, as if it's really nothing at all.

The existence of free energy, cars that run on H_2O, steam diesel injection in heavy vehicles, low-cost medical cures and so on, are all kept safely on the back burner, while the elites are designing their next super yacht and keeping the mob of Rome strictly in their place.

As for 'ETs', the spiritual resurrection of the human race is not high on their agenda. They principally regard us as gene stock, milch cows and generally easily-led and deceived lesser intelligences, which they or their cousins created many millennia ago to do the donkey-work down here on this mud ball Earth. At best, they view Earth as a wildlife park and at worst, as simply a farm open all hours to nick what they need to maintain their own physical or energetic sustenance by stealing your auric energy like psychic vampires of the night. (Many a story and legend thinly veils the truth - 'Hidden in Plain Sight')

Yes, there are higher forces at work who see this planet, may be even this whole solar system, as a school where the duress of it all is character building, development of the Soul. But they mostly hide behind the philosophy of non-interference, neutrality and not wanting to get involved.

When they have, by perhaps generating a prophet or messiah, the faithful followers eventually turn to violence, forcefully converting non-believers or simply eliminating them by massacre or genocide.

Whichever religion, cult or sect, they're all the same breed, same meat and veg, different gravy. Does this come from the primate DNA genes or from the 'off-worlders' who spliced some of their own genetic material into the mix to make humans? They were dedicated colonialists and exploiters of the lands, planets and moons they discovered eons before the human ones in our written 'history'.

Were they missionaries? I don't think so, just entrepreneurs whose ruthless psychology can be seen mirrored in the frontiersman attitudes of J. P.

Morgan and such like, the dynastic families who have governed the world from before the Egyptian dynasties, through the hierarchical kings and brotherhoods of The Knights of Malta, to the ancient bloodlines that defend their right to rule with a rod of iron. Check it out; I am one of this breed, so I know the inside track. I know the 'form' as they would say in a good horse race. No walk-over these guys, they play for real and they don't take prisoners.

Are times a-changing? Maybe. There are lots of bun fights going on for control as I write in 2018, in the USA, the Middle East, SE Asia, Europe and the UK, to name but a few.

These battles, both physical and for 'the mind' are not only from different economic groups seeking advantage, but also from schools of thought with divergent philosophies. We certainly are living in 'interesting times'.

PETER PAGET

Postscript: UFO – Original Update 1980

Just after the completion of this original manuscript in 1980, I was informed of a high-level leak of a classified Russian document, which gave an intriguing inside view of the then-Soviet view of the 'UFO invasion'. The document, which purported to originate from Vladimir Grigorievich Azhazha, deputy director of the Section of Underwater Research, USSR Academy of Sciences, is considered by Western experts to be totally genuine and reveals the following startling information.

According to the Russians, the malfunction on the ill-fated NASA Apollo 13 mission, which was prematurely aborted while on the way to the moon, was instigated by a UFO. The Soviets maintain that Apollo 13 was carrying a small nuclear explosive device designed to provide shock-waves for a geological seismic experiment on the lunar surface after the LEM had taken off from the moon, but at the same time as the nuclear powered Apollo battery unit malfunctioned the nuclear device was also affected.

The Russians further claim that the Western

governments' knowledge of UFO activity is far greater than they openly admit and they suggest that there is evidence that a large extra-terrestrial vessel broke up in Earth's orbit in 1955, of which 10 pieces remain. Two of them were over 100 feet long and weighing in excess of 15 tons, at a range of 1,200 miles up. These had apparently been tracked by radar both by the USSR and the USA and there is some vague suggestion that a cooperative effort could be mounted to retrieve part of the debris using the space shuttle, thereby recovering material without it burning up on re-entry.

The document refers to the subsequent serious nervous breakdown of Buzz Aldrin upon his return from the Apollo II mission, during which it is rumoured the astronauts sighted unidentified space craft in their vicinity on the lunar surface. It is further alleged that Armstrong is at present engaged in secret American investigations into UFO underground activity and that both Warsaw Pact and NATO naval forces have tracked underwater 'unknowns' travelling at speeds of 150 knots, something in excess of 90 knots faster than any known submarine.

They also claim that the French undersea explorer Jacques Piccard, observed a UFO deep in the Mariana Trench during his famous descent. This is an interesting corollary, if true, with regard to information in Chapter 10 of this book from 'Lenston', and subsequent to the communications at that time, another 'extra-terrestrial source' has stated that tectonic movements in the Earth's plates will occur before 1st January 1983.

From the insight given by the Russian leak and born out to some extent by information recently prised from the CIA by the 'Ground Saucer Watch' of Arizona, it would seem that reports that emerged from both sides of the Iron Curtain referring to grounded UFOs containing the bodies of diminutive operators may well be more than just moonshine.

Both NATO and Soviet nuclear installations would appear to have been visited by the UFOs and an inexplicable capacity to neutralise them and take out electronic systems has been demonstrated by this unknown technology.

It would seem well established now within the higher echelons of both sides that Big Brother is watching you.

Epilogue 2018: 'Brave New World'

Dear Reader,

This book must go to press now even though there is much more I would wish to say. But I am between a rock and the hard place on these further revelations as I have to observe both the UK and US security regulations, the 30 and 50-year rule, classifications of 'Restricted', 'Top Secret' and in the UK 'Most Secret'. However, I have tried in this rewritten work to follow on from my two previous works, my autobiography, "*Secret Life of a Spook*" (2016) and "*The Welsh Triangle Revisited*" (2018) recently published.

The reissue of "*UFO-UK Updated 2018*" allows me to work in important insights that you need to know. It is a more negative book than the original 1980 edition, but I was much younger then. However, I don't want you to go away just shaking your head, blown away by how difficult matters have been on this planet and in this solar system. In fact, they are improving.

There are strong, powerful forces at work and enlightened beings working to bring about a resolve here on this planet and indeed in this section of the galactic wing, but you have been in the "B" stream for a very long time and totally taken advantage of.

Be aware from the constant and obsessive efforts made by both 'ET' and governments to keep matters hidden, confused and secret, that the one single power that blows this wide open is the dissemination of the truth; the simple truth.

If a regime is operating within a cloak of secrecy and illusion, it has weaknesses that only that obscuration hides. The 'ET' forces on both 'sides' are very limited in number; their attitude is often stale, out of date and limited to what they have practiced for hundreds, if not thousands, of years. Advanced technology when so automated, as theirs is, leads to weakness of character in the operators who run it. They depend a lot on quantum light AI (Artificial Intelligence Computers) and as in their craft, use fibre optics rather than conductive wiring. The AI listens all the time, to them, to you, to me. We are all interacting with it and can affect its decisions. You have a stake in this and the AI with its minions and racial groups has the betterment of all at its heart, because it was built that way many millennia ago.

So exercise your power. Wake up. Don't be a useless thing. Take control of your personal life, your thoughts, your motivations and rise to the level of the gods you are and from whom you were made (Sumerian legends). This is indeed a 'Brave New World' and all your dreams can be fulfilled, but only if you are the master of them and not just a copycat transformer to repeat the mantras of others, no matter who or what they may be.

I have worked with all of these groups and forces for over half a century and live to inspire you to be better, do better and be better informed. I trust I will, in time, succeed with that.

My next, and may be last book, will be, 'The Dark Triangle', out for 2019.

Blessings,

Peter Paget, 2018

WHERE TO FIND PETER ONLINE

Peter Paget's live presentations can be found on his website, www.peterpaget.com

His Facebook page can be found at www.Facebook.com/PeterPagetDisclosure

Various presentations can also be found on YouTube, sometimes under distribution from Project Camelot, Kerry Cassidy or Miles Johnston, the Bases Project.

To get in touch by email, write to peterpaget2012@yahoo.co.uk

Note: Peter cannot answer Facebook messages due to volume of traffic.

Other Books by Peter Paget

The Welsh Triangle — Granada/Panther, 1979
UFO-UK — New English Library, 1980
The Welsh Triangle — French Edition, 1981
Secret Life of a Spook — 2016
The Welsh Triangle Revisited — 2018
UFO-UK Updated — 2018
The Dark Triangle — Expected 2019

Also contributed to:
The Ufonauts — Panther, 1979
The Uninvited — Star, 1979
Crop Circles Revealed — Light Technology, 2001

Printed in Great Britain
by Amazon